PAPER GALAXY

Out-of-This-World Projects to Cut, Fold & Paste

M. D. Prins

STERLING PUBLISHING CO., INC.
NEW YORK

Library of Congress Cataloging-in-Publication Data

Prins, M. D.
    Paper galaxy : out-of-this-world projects to cut, fold & paste / M.D. Prins.
        p. cm.
    Includes index.
    ISBN 1-4027-2131-5
        1. Paper work—Juvenile literature. [1. Paper work. 2. Handicraft.] I. Title:
Out-of-this-world projects to cut, fold & paste. II. Title: Projects to cut, fold, and paste.
III. Title.

TT870.P77 2005
736'.98—dc22

                                                                2005049033

10 9 8 7 6 5 4 3 2 1

Published by Sterling Publishing Co., Inc.
387 Park Avenue South, New York, NY 10016
© 2005 by Michael D. Prins
Distributed in Canada by Sterling Publishing
c/o Canadian Manda Group, 165 Dufferin Street
Toronto, Ontario, Canada M6K 3H6
Distributed in Great Britain by Chrysalis Books Group PLC
The Chrysalis Building, Bramley Road, London W10 6SP, England
Distributed in Australia by Capricorn Link (Australia) Pty. Ltd.
P.O. Box 704, Windsor, NSW 2756, Australia

Printed in China

Sterling ISBN 1-4027-2131-5

For information about custom editions, special sales, premium and
corporate purchases, please contact Sterling Special Sales
Department at 800-805-5489 or specialsales@sterlingpub.com.

Contents

GENERAL INSTRUCTIONS

PROJECTS

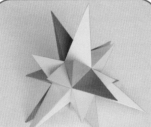

Welcome to the Paper Galaxy. With the patterns and instructions in this book, you will be able to make fantastic three-dimensional creations using only paper, scissors, and glue. After you have built a few of the stars and other creations, you will have your own paper galaxy. The projects in this book will provide

1. White glue or craft glue, scissors, and a pencil are some of the supplies needed.

hours and hours of creative fun. The simpler and smaller projects will probably take about an hour; the larger projects, up to 5 or 6 hours. Most will take 2 or 3 hours. After making the projects in this book, you will know how to invent your very own variations and creations. The possibilities are cosmic!

Tools and Supplies

You will need:

- scissors
- strong glue such as craft glue or white glue suitable for paper (Photo 1)
- sharp pencil
- ruler
- thin cardboard, about the thickness of looseleaf separators or manila folders

- tracing paper, or any thin white paper that you can see through
- card-stock paper for making templates or patterns (optional; see Transfer Method 3). Card stock is paper that is the weight of note cards, which is heavier than the usual photocopy-weight paper
- needle and thread for loops with which to hang stars and other creations (optional)

The above tools are needed for all the projects. A craft knife, such as an X-Acto knife, might be useful on 2 or 3 projects for cutting out small areas, but it isn't essential. If you are not allowed to use a craft knife yet, ask an adult to help you for those parts or use scissors.

Paper for Projects

Many kinds of paper can be used to make the paper creations in this book. Use whatever colors and textures suit your imagination. Generally, paper about the thickness and stiffness of normal office letter-weight paper or copy machine paper works best. Some examples of paper that works well: colored copy paper, magazine covers, old calendars, advertisements, old posters, used envelopes, and stiff wrapping paper (Photo 2). Magazine pages and normal wrapping paper are usually too thin and flimsy. They bend too easily.

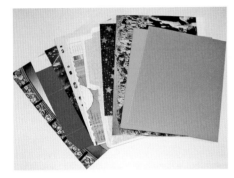

2. Some types of paper for projects: copy paper, magazine covers, and heavy gift wrap paper.

For each project, read the instructions through to find out what kind of paper you need for that project. Assemble your materials before starting. Plan which colors will be used in which parts.

Transferring the Patterns

The patterns in this book must be transferred to the project paper you have selected. There are three methods for doing this. All three work very well; just choose the one that is easiest for you. Illustration 3 shows a typical base pattern, complete with glue flaps that will be used to assemble the pattern piece and attach it to other pieces.

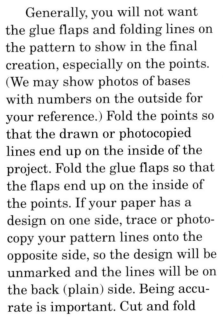

glue flap

3. A typical base pattern piece. Shaded trapezoid areas are glue flaps.

Generally, you will not want the glue flaps and folding lines on the pattern to show in the final creation, especially on the points. (We may show photos of bases with numbers on the outside for your reference.) Fold the points so that the drawn or photocopied lines end up on the inside of the project. Fold the glue flaps so that the flaps end up on the inside of the points. If your paper has a design on one side, trace or photocopy your pattern lines onto the opposite side, so the design will be unmarked and the lines will be on the back (plain) side. Being accurate is important. Cut and fold

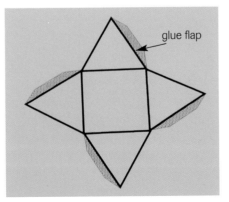

glue flap

4. Method 1, a pattern that was photocopied directly onto project paper.

exactly on the lines so that your creations will fit together perfectly.

Transfer Method 1: With Photocopier or Scanner

The first method transfers the pattern from the book directly to your project paper using a standard office photocopying machine (Photo 4). White or colored paper can be used. After copying, you can decorate the paper with markers, crayons, or paint before cutting and folding the pattern. The copy machine can also be used to enlarge or reduce the patterns to any size. (If you enlarge or reduce, be sure that you keep the horizontal and vertical dimensions in exactly the same ratio.) Copying the pattern also can be done by scanning it and printing it on your home computer. If you enlarge the base of a project a certain amount, be sure to enlarge all the other project pieces the same amount.

If you use Transfer Method 2 or 3 to copy the patterns, work with a very sharp pencil, so that your lines are right at the edge of the cut-out template.

Transfer Method 2: Using Templates of Geometric Shapes

The second method transfers the patterns from the book to your paper using tracing paper and cardboard to make a template of each geometric shape. (A template is a pattern.) This can be done in five easy steps, without the use of a photocopier.

1. Trace one of each geometric shape in the pattern piece (not including the glue flaps) onto tracing paper. For the pattern shown in Photo 4, you would trace a square and a triangle.

2. Cut out each shape from the tracing paper and glue it to thin cardboard (Photo 5).

3. Create a cardboard template of each shape by cutting out each traced shape.

4. On your selected project paper, position and trace around the cardboard templates to recreate the pattern in the book. For example, for the pattern shown, trace the square template once in the center and trace the triangle template 4 times so that one side of each triangle is lined up on each edge of the square (Photo 6).

5. Draw in the glue flaps on the pattern piece as shown in the book by hand-sketching (these do not have to be exact; Photo 7).

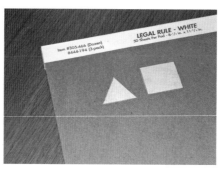

5. Method 2, two tracings of pattern shapes that were glued to cardboard for use as templates.

6. Method 2, tracing a cardboard template onto the project paper to recreate the pattern piece.

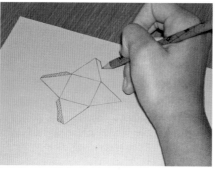

7. Method 2, drawing on the glue flaps to the pattern piece.

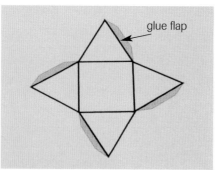

8. Method 3, a pattern piece photo-copied onto card stock.

Transfer Method 3: Making a Template of a Whole Pattern Piece

The third method transfers the pattern from the book to your template paper using a copy machine (or home computer, scanner, and printer) so you can make a card-stock paper template of an entire pattern piece. This can be done in five easy steps.

1. Load the copier (or printer) with the card-stock paper. Photocopy the pattern from the book onto card-stock paper (Photo 8).

2. Create a card-stock template of the entire pattern by cutting around the outsides of the pattern piece, not including the glue flaps (cut off the glue flaps).

3. On the back side of your selected paper, trace around the card-stock template (Photo 9) you created in Step 2.

4. Add any interior pattern lines using a ruler (Photo 10).

5. Draw the glue flaps for the pattern as shown in Photo 7 by hand-sketching; glue flaps do not have to be exact.

Cutting, Folding, Gluing, and Paper Choices

- Start with some of the simpler projects near the front of the book, like the Sunburst. After you have mastered a few of the simpler projects, you will be ready to do any of the others.

- After copying the pattern pieces to your chosen project paper, cut out the pattern pieces from your chosen paper, including the glue flaps, and follow the project instructions to assemble.

■ Usually, you will want to fold the copies of the pattern so that the drawn or photocopied lines and the glue flaps end up inside the three-dimensional point or base (Photo 11). Sometimes you may want to keep the lines on the outside for guidance (for example, on a base that will be covered entirely by points later on). You also will see numbers on the outside of some bases in our photos, for your guidance.

■ Test-fit pieces together before gluing. If necessary, make small adjustments to folds for perfect fit.

■ Each glue flap needs to be held for a minute or two after gluing until the glue sets. Shiny paper usually needs to be held slightly longer than matte paper (paper that is not shiny). Craft glue works better than normal white glue on shiny paper. On some of the bases, you might want to glue one-half or one-third of the glue flaps and then take a

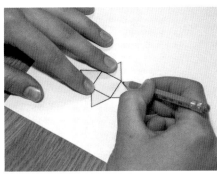

9. Method 3, a card-stock template is traced onto the wrong (back) side of the project paper.

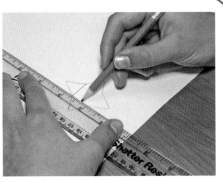

10. Method 3, interior lines of the pattern are drawn.

break to let them dry before continuing.

■ On the star projects, the base is often covered completely by the points when the star is finished. Still, it is a good idea to use the same color paper for the base as for the points, so that any small gaps between the base and the points are not noticeable.

Displaying Your Projects

Your paper creations can be displayed either sitting on a flat surface or hanging. Most can sit anywhere—for example, on a bookshelf. To hang a star, use a threaded needle to make a small hole through one of the points.

Use thread or hobby wire to make a hanging loop that goes through the needle hole. Put a small hook in the ceiling. (You may need to get an adult to help you.) Use another thread to attach the hanging loop to the ceiling hook. If you want to hang several stars, you can attach two ceiling hooks or screw eyes on opposite sides of the room. Run string, sturdy thread, or fishing line between the two hooks and then hang stars all along the string. Stars painted with metallic paint after you have assembled them make interesting decorative items for any room in the house. Many also make great Christmas decorations (Photo 12).

11. Assembling a pattern piece. Left: A folded pattern piece. Middle: With one glue flap glued. Right: Finished piece. Lines are drawn very dark for emphasis here.

12. A group of completed projects.

Geometric Shapes

This book is full of geometric shapes. You might find it fun to learn a bit about them. The names of these shapes are easy to learn. Two-dimensional closed shapes with straight sides are called polygons. Each polygon has a name that tells you how many sides it has. The names are based on Greek words or roots: *tri-* for three; *tetra-* for four, *penta-* for five, *hexa-* for six, *hepta-* for seven, and *octa-* for eight sides. Polygons are flat shapes that you can draw on paper.

The polygons shown in Illustration 13 are special polygons called regular polygons, because in each one, all the sides are equal to each other and all the angles are equal to each other. For example, in a regular tetragon (square), all the angles are 90°.

We also use some irregular polygons (polygons with unequal sides) in the book (see Illustration 14).

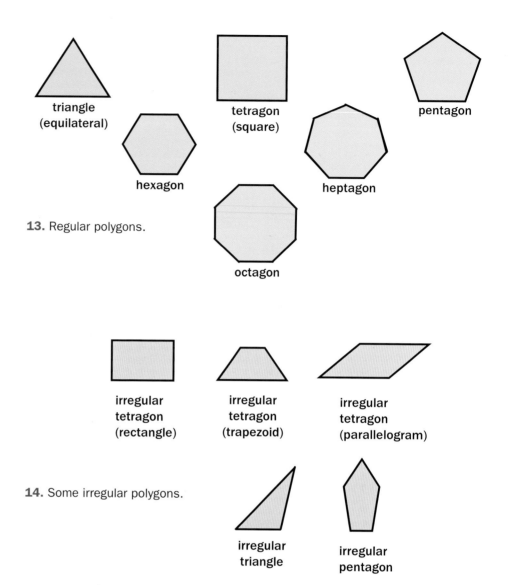

13. Regular polygons.

triangle (equilateral)
tetragon (square)
pentagon
hexagon
heptagon
octagon

14. Some irregular polygons.

irregular tetragon (rectangle)
irregular tetragon (trapezoid)
irregular tetragon (parallelogram)
irregular triangle
irregular pentagon

Pentagonal pyramid point and dodecahedron base from Dodec Twinkler project.

Truncated pyramid base and a point from Four July Sky project.

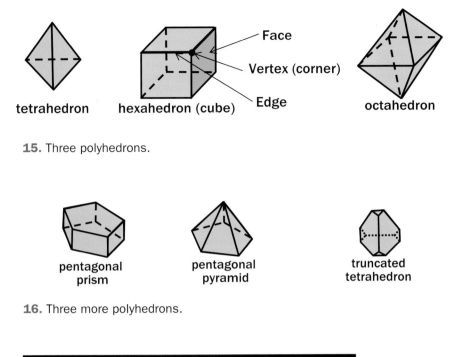

tetrahedron   hexahedron (cube)   octahedron

Face
Vertex (corner)
Edge

15. Three polyhedrons.

pentagonal prism   pentagonal pyramid   truncated tetrahedron

16. Three more polyhedrons.

A closed solid that has a flat polygon for each face is called a polyhedron. The polyhedron's name usually tells you the number of faces. Again, these are based on Greek roots: *tetra-* for four faces, *hexa-* for six faces, *octa-* for eight faces, *dodeca-* for twelve faces, and *icosa-* for twenty faces; see Illustration 15 for some examples. *Hedron* means face in Greek.

A prism is a special polyhedron that has two end faces that are parallel, identical polygons; all its other faces are parallelograms or rectangles. (A rectangle is actually a special type of parallelogram with 90° angles). A pyramid is a polyhedron that has a polygon for its base; all of its other sides are triangles that meet at a single vertex. Some additional polyhedrons are formed by truncating (cutting off the corners) of other polyhedrons (see Illustration 16).

The Base Geometry Summary at the end of the book provides additional information on the polyhedrons used in the Paper Galaxy projects.

Cube base from Sirius project.

Pentagonal prism base and a square pyramid point from Pentacle project.

Icosahedron base and a hexagonal pyramid point from Mira Ceti project.

SUNBURST

Great for beginners, the Sunburst is a fun and easy project. Hundreds of great variations can be made from this same basic pattern.

Sunburst 1

1. Refer to the General Instructions section of the book for copying patterns. After copying the Sunburst base pattern to your chosen project paper, cut out the entire pattern, including the glue flaps. Fold on all lines. Glue each flap, one at a time, to the adjacent triangle, and then close the base by attaching flaps c to edges d. When fully assembled, the base should look as shown in Photo 1, left. The geometric shape of the base is an icosahedron: a solid figure that has 20 faces. Each face is an equilateral triangle.

2. Make the 20 points by making 20 copies of the pattern for Point 3 onto your chosen project paper or papers. Cut out each point pattern, including the glue flaps. Fold on all lines. Assemble each point by gluing flap a to the opposite triangle at edge e. An assembled point should look as shown on the right in Photo 1. You can make all 20 points the same color (Photo 2) or you can make 4 points in each of 5 different colors of paper, as shown in Photo 3.

3. Attach the points to the base. For each point, place glue on the three b glue flaps; then stick the point to one face of the base. If you have 5 different colors of point, you can use the numbers shown on the base as a guide for arranging the points so that two points of the same color are never adjacent (right next to each other).

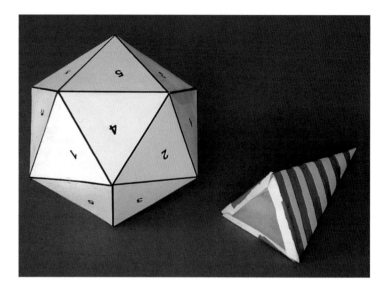

1. Sunburst base (for Sunburst 1 and 2) and a point. Numbers indicate which point to glue in that triangle (for Sunburst 2) or which color or pattern to use (Sunburst 1).

2. Sunburst 1 on plaid-painted paper.

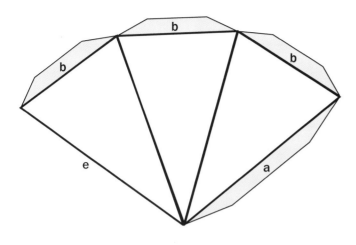

Point 3. Make 20 for Sunburst 1. Make 4 for Sunburst 2.

3. Sunburst 1 in which 4 of the point pattern (Point 3) were cut out of 5 different paper designs.

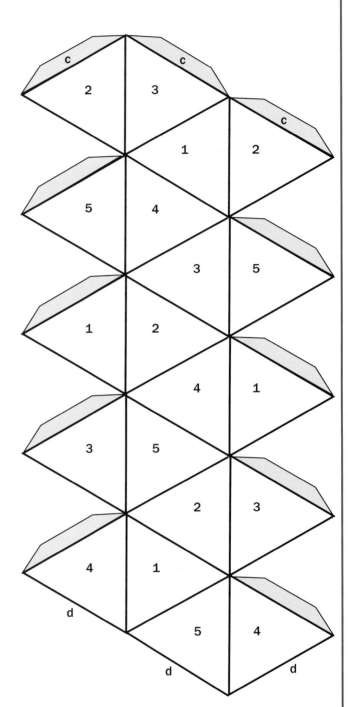

Icosahedron base: Make 1 base for Sunburst 1 or 2. Numbers are guides for point placement.

Sunburst 2

1. To make Sunburst 2, make the same base as for Sunburst 1.

2. Make four of Point 1, four of Point 2, four of Point 3, four of Point 4, and four of Point 5, instead of making 20 of Point 3. See Step 2 of Sunburst 1 for how to cut and assemble a point.

3. Glue the points to the base according to the numbers on each face of the base: Attach Point 1 to each base face labeled with a 1, etc.

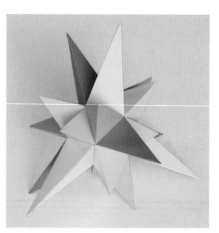

4. Sunburst 2, with each point type cut of a different color of paper.

5. Sunburst 2, with all the points cut from paint-spattered paper.

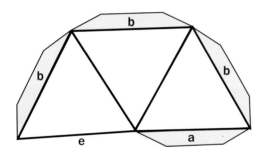

Point 1. Make 4 for Sunburst 2.

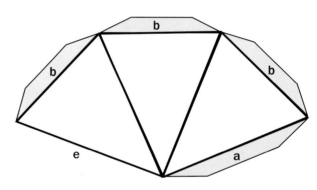

Point 2. Make 4 for Sunburst 2.

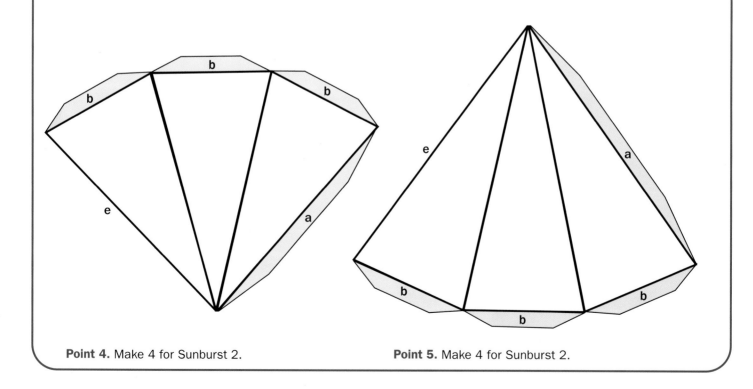

Point 4. Make 4 for Sunburst 2.

Point 5. Make 4 for Sunburst 2.

Mercury is fast. It hurtles through space at 30 miles per second to make its trip around the Sun in just 88 earth days.

1. Refer to the General Instructions section of the book for copying patterns. Make the icosahedron base, following the Sunburst base instructions on page 10. Parts of the base will show when complete, so fold the base so that the pattern lines end up on the inside. Choose a paper color for the base that will look good with the colors you choose for the points. Our example uses silver paper for the base and gold paper for the points.

2. Make 20 of Point 1. First copy the pattern 20 times onto your chosen project paper. Cut out the entire pattern, including the glue flaps. Fold on all lines. Assemble each point by gluing flap a to the opposite triangle at edge e.

3. Use the remaining 3 glue flaps on each point to glue each point to one face of the base. The point should be rotated when gluing so that each corner of the point is at the center of an edge of a triangle on the base (see Photo 1).

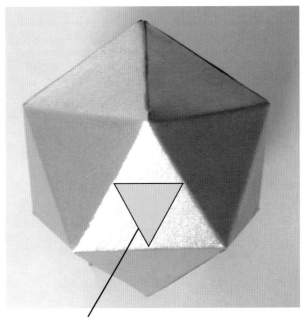

1. Area covered by a point.

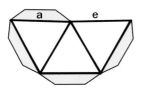

Point 1. Make 20.

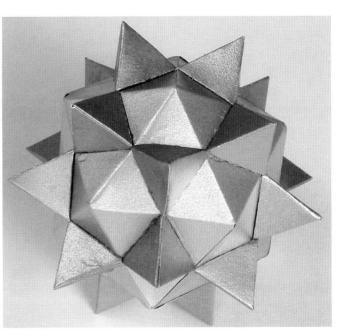

2. The completed Mercury.

The Tetra-Twelve is easy to make. Spin it round and around; it looks different from each direction.

1. Refer to the General Instructions section of the book for copying patterns. To make the tetrahedron base, copy the base pattern to your chosen project paper and cut out the entire pattern, including the glue flaps. Fold on all lines. Glue flap c to the adjacent triangle at edge d and let dry. Then complete and close the base by gluing the last triangle onto the remaining 2 glue flaps. This base is a regular tetrahedron. A tetrahedron is a solid that has 4 sides (or faces, as we say sometimes). The base is a "regular" tetrahedron because each face of the tetrahedron is an identical equilateral triangle.

2. Make 4 of the intermediate tetrahedrons. For each, copy and cut out the entire pattern and fold on all lines. Glue flap f to the adjacent triangle at edge g, and let dry. These tetrahedrons have one open side.

3. Attach the 4 intermediate tetrahedrons to the base (see Photo 1). Put glue on each of the intermediate tetrahedron's 3 glue flaps, and use these to attach the open side of the intermediate tetrahedron to one face of the base tetrahedron.

4. To make the 12 points, cut out each entire pattern and fold on all lines. Glue flap a to the opposite triangle at edge e.

5. To attach the points, put glue on each point's 3 glue flaps and attach to any face of an intermediate tetrahedron. Be sure to orient each point so that glue flap b is at the bottom of the intermediate tetrahedron face (where it attaches to the base tetrahedron).

The Tetra-Twelve can be made in any size by changing the size of the equilateral triangles on the base and on the intermediate tetrahedrons, making the sides of the pentagon pattern for the point the same length as the sides of the base triangle.

1. Tetrahedron base (lower left); base with 4 intermediate tetrahedrons attached (center), and a point (right).

2. The completed Tetra-Twelve, made with 3 points in each of 4 different paper colors.

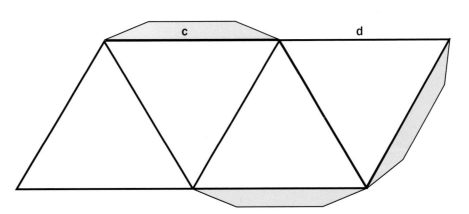

Tetrahedron base for Tetra-Twelve. Make 1.

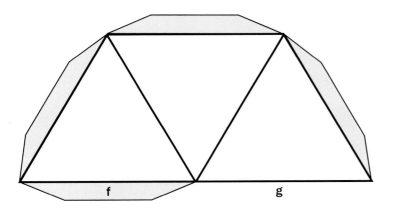

Intermediate tetrahedron. Make 4.

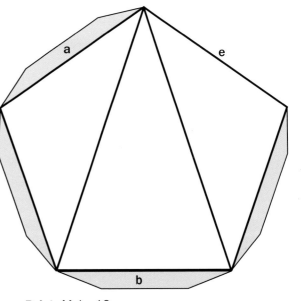

Point. Make 12.

Twisted and tangled, the Twisted Twelve looks difficult but is actually quite easy to make. The types of pieces and construction are the same as those of the Tetra-Twelve, but the shapes of the intermediate tetrahedrons and points are different.

1. Refer to the General Instructions section of the book for copying patterns. To make the tetrahedron base, after copying the base pattern to your chosen project paper, cut out the entire pattern, including the glue flaps. Fold on all lines. Glue flap c to edge d and let dry. Then complete and close the base by gluing the 2 remaining glue flaps onto the remaining base triangle.

2. Make 4 of the intermediate tetrahedrons. For each, copy and cut out the entire pattern, including glue flaps, and fold on all lines. Glue flap f to the opposite triangle at edge g, and let dry. Note that these intermediate tetrahedrons are short and flat.

3. To attach each of the 4 intermediate tetrahedrons to the base, put glue on each of the 3 remaining flaps, and use these flaps to attach the open side of each intermediate tetrahedron to a face of the base tetrahedron.

4. To make the 12 points, copy and cut out the entire pattern for each, including glue flaps, and fold on all lines. Glue flap a to the opposite triangle at edge e and let dry.

5. To attach the points, put glue on each of the 3 remaining glue flaps and attach the point to any face of an intermediate tetrahedron. Make sure the point is oriented so that glue flap b is at the bottom of the intermediate tetrahedron face (where it attaches to the base tetrahedron).

1. Left to right: tetrahedron base, intermediate tetrahedron, and typical point.

2. The completed Twisted Twelve.

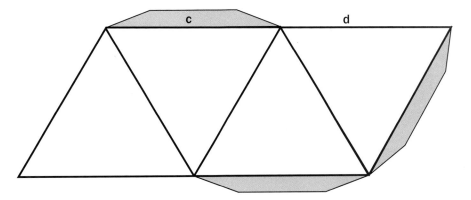

Tetrahedron base for Twisted Twelve. Make 1.

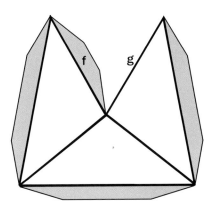

Intermediate tetrahedron. Make 4.

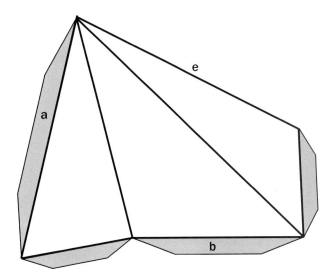

Point. Make 12.

CHRISTMAS STAR

The Christmas Star shows up in decorations everywhere at Christmas. Make your own with this simple pattern.

1. Refer to the General Instructions section of the book for copying patterns. To make each of the 5 points, after copying the point pattern to your chosen project paper, cut out each entire point, including the glue flaps. Fold on all lines. Complete each point by gluing flap a to the opposite triangle at edge e. A completed point should look like the point photo (Photo 1).

2. Connect the 5 points together as follows: Glue the two flaps b of one point to the two flaps c of the next point (with both flaps inside the point so that they do not show). Continue around in this fashion, connecting flaps b to flaps c, until all 5 points are connected. The fifth point is attached to both the fourth and the first point. To help orient the points correctly, notice that all points d end up at the center of the star.

2. The completed Christmas Star.

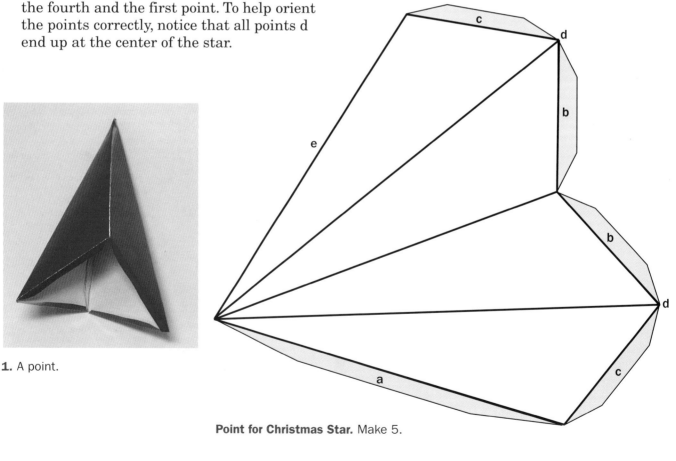

1. A point.

Point for Christmas Star. Make 5.

DODEC TWINKLER

The Dodec Twinkler looks impressive, but it is easy to make. Here are two versions.

Dodec Twinkler 1

1. Refer to the General Instructions section of the book for copying patterns. To make the base, copy the base pattern to your chosen paper, and cut out the entire base, including the glue flaps. Fold on all lines. Glue each flap, one at a time, to the adjacent pentagon (the 5-sided figure) on the base. When fully assembled, the base should look as shown in Photo 1. This base is a dodecahedron. A dodecahedron is a solid that has 12 faces; each face is an identical regular pentagon. A regular pentagon is a pentagon whose sides are of equal length and whose angles are all equal.

2. To make the 12 points, copy twelve of the Point 1 pattern. Cut out each entire point, including the glue flaps. Fold on all lines. Assemble each point by gluing flap a to the opposite triangle at edge e. An assembled point should look like the one in Photo 1.

3. To attach the points to the base, place glue on the 5 remaining flaps of each point, and then glue it to one face of the base.

2. Completed Dodec Twinkler 1.

1. Point for Dodec Twinkler 1 (left) and base.

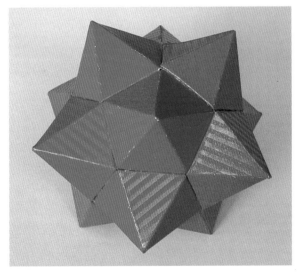

3. Completed Dodec Twinkler 2.

Dodec Twinkler 2

Follow the instructions for Dodec Twinkler 1, but use the Point 2 pattern instead of the Point 1 pattern.

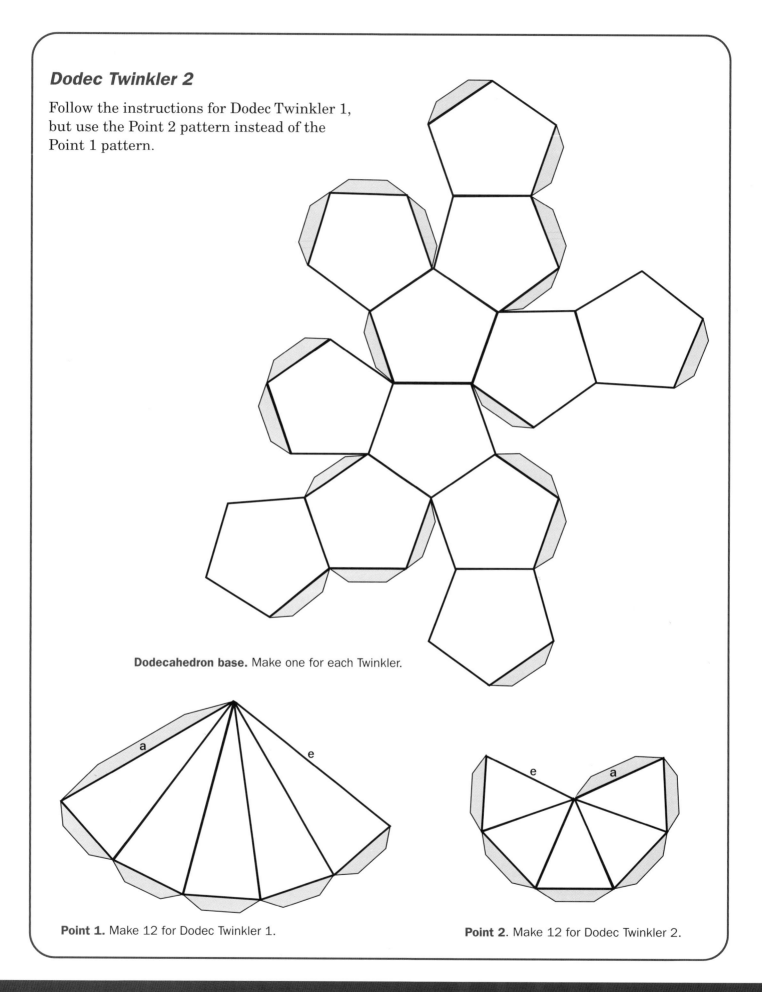

Dodecahedron base. Make one for each Twinkler.

Point 1. Make 12 for Dodec Twinkler 1.

Point 2. Make 12 for Dodec Twinkler 2.

ANDROMEDA GALAXY

About 2 000 000 light-years away, the Andromeda Galaxy is the nearest neighbor to our own Milky Way. It is a spiral galaxy (like our Milky Way), and it is about 200 000 light-years across. Use this pattern to make your own just slightly smaller model. The paper you select for this project should be the same color on both sides.

1. See the General Instructions for copying patterns. To make the hexagonal prism base, copy and cut out the entire pattern from your chosen paper, including the glue flaps. Fold on all lines. Attach each rectangle on the base to the adjacent rectangle, using the green g glue flaps. Complete and close the prism by folding and gluing the lower hexagon onto the 5 blue glue flaps.

2. Make the 12 Andromeda Galaxy arms: six of Arm 1 and six of Arm 2. First copy the patterns; then cut out each entire arm, including the glue flap. Fold on the line between the arm shape and the glue flap. For Arm 1 arms, fold the glue flaps forward; for Arm 2 arms, fold the glue flaps backward. If you want to paint or decorate your galaxy, do this now. Decorate arms on both sides. Try glitter or glitter paint to create a starry effect.

3. All arms attach to the rectangular sides of the prism base. Glue each Arm 1 to a rectangular side of the base at edge a (Photo 2). Glue each Arm 2 to a rectangular side of the base at edge b. All arms should spiral in the same direction. If an arm does not, reverse the direction in which the arm's glue flap is folded.

1. Two arms and a hexagonal prism base.

2. Andromeda base with one arm attached.

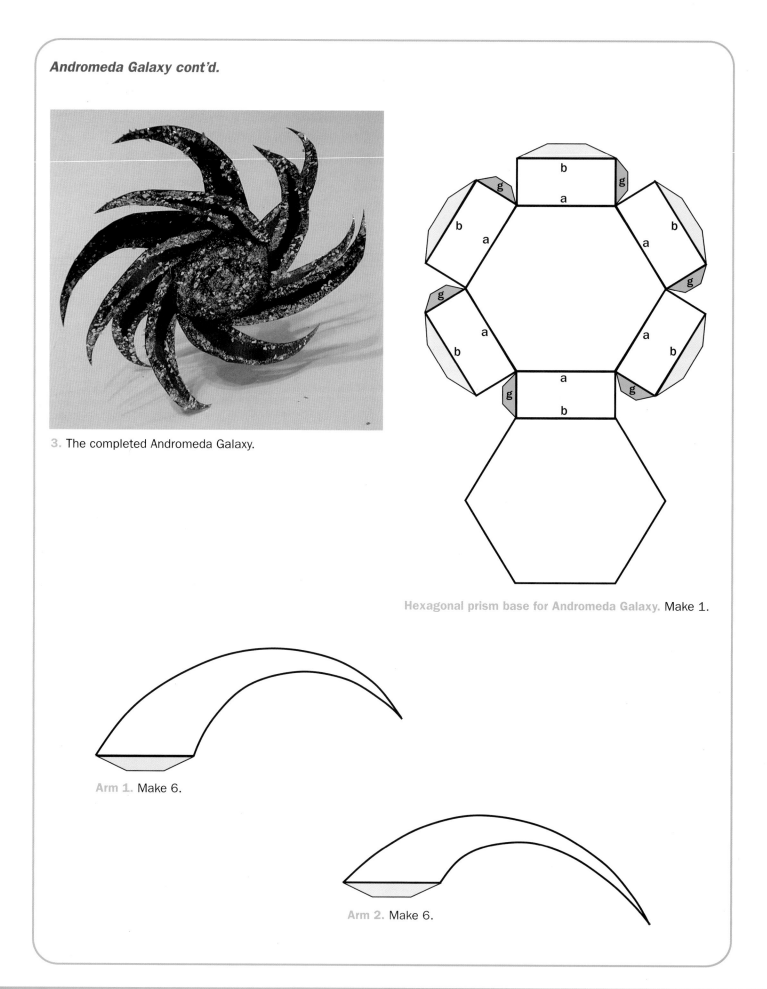

3. The completed Andromeda Galaxy.

Hexagonal prism base for Andromeda Galaxy. Make 1.

Arm 1. Make 6.

Arm 2. Make 6.

Make the magical Pentacle in three easy steps.
Then get fancier with a Double Pentacle.

Pentacle

1. Refer to the General Instructions section of the book for copying patterns. To make the base, copy the pentagonal prism base pattern to your chosen paper and cut out the entire pattern, including the glue flaps. Fold on all lines except the dotted lines. Glue each green g flap onto the adjacent square of the base. Complete and close the base by gluing the unglued pentagon onto the remaining glue flaps.

2. Make five of Point 1. For each, copy and cut out the entire point pattern and fold on all lines. Glue flap a to the opposite triangle at edge e to complete each point.

3. To attach the points to the base, glue each point to a square face of the base.

1. Base and point for Pentacle.

2. The completed Pentacle.

3. The completed Double Pentacle.

Double Pentacle

1. Make the same pentagonal prism base as for the Pentacle; see Step 1 of Pentacle.

2. Use the Point 2 pattern to make 10 points. Make each as follows: cut out the entire point pattern and fold on all lines. Glue flap a to the opposite triangle at edge e to complete the point.

3. To attach the points to the base, glue 2 points to each square face of the base, one on each side of the dotted line. Orient the 2 points on each face in opposite directions, as shown in the Double Pentacle photo on page 23.

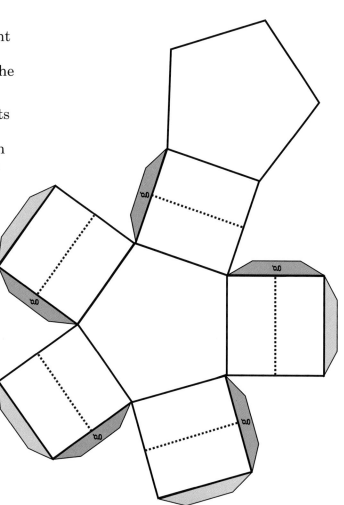

Pentagonal base. Make 1 for the Pentacle or for the Double Pentacle.

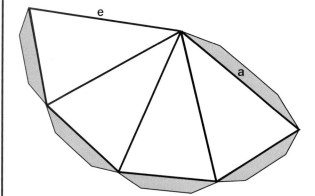

Point 1. Make 5 for the Pentacle.

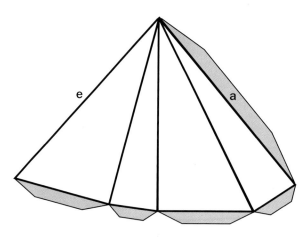

Point 2. Make 10 for the Double Pentacle.

Capella is actually a double star that is 150 times brighter than the Sun. Use this pattern to make your own version of Capella.

1. Refer to the General Instructions section of the book for copying patterns. To make the two halves of the base, copy 2 of the hexagonal pyramid half-base pattern to your chosen paper and cut out each pattern, including the glue flaps. Fold on all lines except the dotted lines. Complete each half-base pyramid by gluing flap c to the opposite triangle at edge d.

2. To attach the two halves of the base together, use the remaining glue flaps to connect the bottoms of the two pyramids. To do this, glue one flap from each half together and let dry. Then glue the other 5 flaps. See Photo 1 for the assembled base.

3. Twelve points are required in total. Three different patterns are provided. The star can be made with any number of each of the three types of point to make up the 12 points. The Capella Star shown in the photos is made with two of Point 1, six of Point 2, and four of Point 3. After copying the patterns of the points you have selected, cut out each entire point pattern, including the glue flaps. Fold on all lines. Complete each point by gluing flap a to the opposite triangle at edge e.

4. The points attach to the base in the areas below the dotted line that are marked with an X. The points must be oriented so that edge b on the point is at edge b on the base. To make the Capella Star pictured, make 2 of Point 1, and attach one Point 1 to each pyramid half base so the points are on opposite sides of the base. On either side of each of these Point 1's, attach a Point 2. Next to each of the four attached Point 2's, attach a Point 3. Attach a Point 2 in the two remaining open spaces. Photos 2 and 3 show two Capellas.

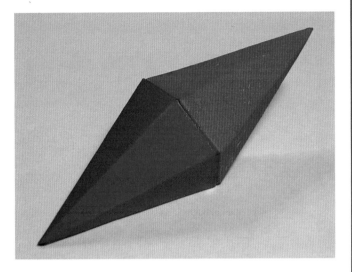

1. Pyramid base with its two halves connected.

2. The completed Capella Star.

3. A spray-painted Capella.

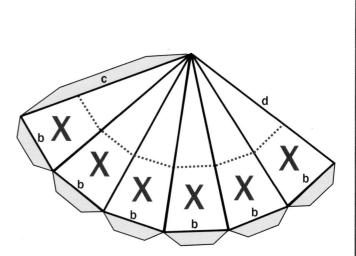

The hexagonal pyramid half-base pattern for the Capella Star. Make 2 for the base.

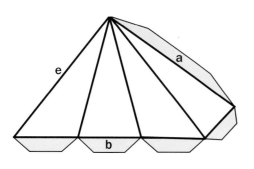

Point 1.

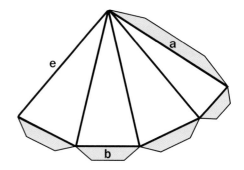

Point 2.

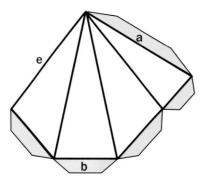

Point 3.

HOT-AIR BALLOON

Let your imagination soar through the clouds with this dreamy Hot Air Balloon. This scale model looks impressive, but is easy to make.

1. Refer to the General Instructions section of the book for copying patterns. To make the 10 segments (parts) of the balloon, copy and cut out the entire pattern of each, including the glue flaps. Fold over the glue flaps at the edge of each balloon segment.

2. Make the balloon by gluing the 10 segments together, using the glue flaps of one segment to attach it to the next segment. When you align the edges of the segments to attach them, the segments will curve to the shape of a balloon. This works best if you hold two segments with their pointy ends up and glue the 3 top glue flaps of one segment to the smooth edge of the next segment. Let the glue dry briefly. Then glue 3 more glue flaps from the first segment to the second one and let dry, etc., until the two segments are fully connected, as shown in Photo 1. Continue adding segments to the structure until all segments are connected. The tenth segment will be connected to both the ninth and the first segments to complete the balloon.

3. To make the basket, cut out the entire basket pattern, including the glue flaps, but be sure to keep the circular base attached to the band. Bend the band around the base so that the band is two layers thick all around and the circle that the band makes is the same size as the circular base. Glue the band to itself; then bend the circular base up and glue the glue flaps in place on the band. Note that the top of the basket will be slightly larger than the bottom of the basket. Attach the basket to the balloon with 4 strings. If you want your balloon to sit on a shelf for display, saturate thick strings with glue and lay them out straight to dry. When dry, glue the strings to the inside of balloon and to the inside of the basket.

One type of paper that looks good for the balloon is multi-colored striped paper. To make the stripes go around the balloon, copy each segment onto the paper with its long sides perpendicular (at 90°) to the stripes. Make sure that the tops of all segments are aligned at the edge of the same stripe on the paper (see Photo 2).

1. Two segments glued together, seen from inside.

2. A completed Hot Air Balloon, made with striped paper. Segments were cut perpendicular to stripes on paper.

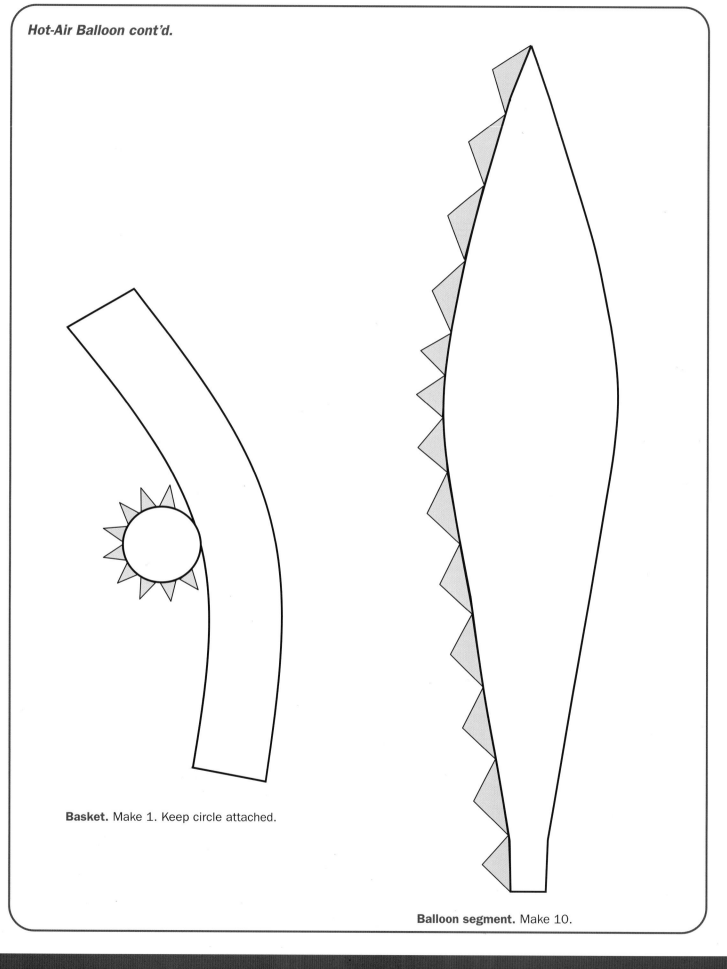

Basket. Make 1. Keep circle attached.

Balloon segment. Make 10.

This Beta Orionis star is named after a blue-white star in the Orion constellation.

1. Refer to the General Instructions section of the book for copying patterns. To make the base, copy the base pattern to your chosen paper, and cut out the entire pattern, including the glue flaps. Fold on all lines. Glue the outer triangle 1's to each other with their unlabeled glue flaps, and glue the outer triangle 2's to each other with their unlabeled glue flaps. Then close the base by gluing flaps c to the triangles on the opposite side of the pattern at edges d. The base should look as shown in Photo 1 when complete.

2. Make 24 points, twelve of Point 1 and twelve of Point 2. Cut out the entire point pattern, including the glue flaps. Fold on all lines. Complete each point by attaching glue flap a to the opposite triangle at edge e. The template for Point 2 is the flipped-over template for Point 1.

3. Use the remaining 3 glue flaps on each point to attach the point to a face of the base. Glue a Point 1 to each triangle face marked with a 1; glue a Point 2 to each face marked with a 2.

1. Base (at top) and 3 points.

2. Front view of the completed Beta Orionis.

3. Top view of the completed Beta Orionis.

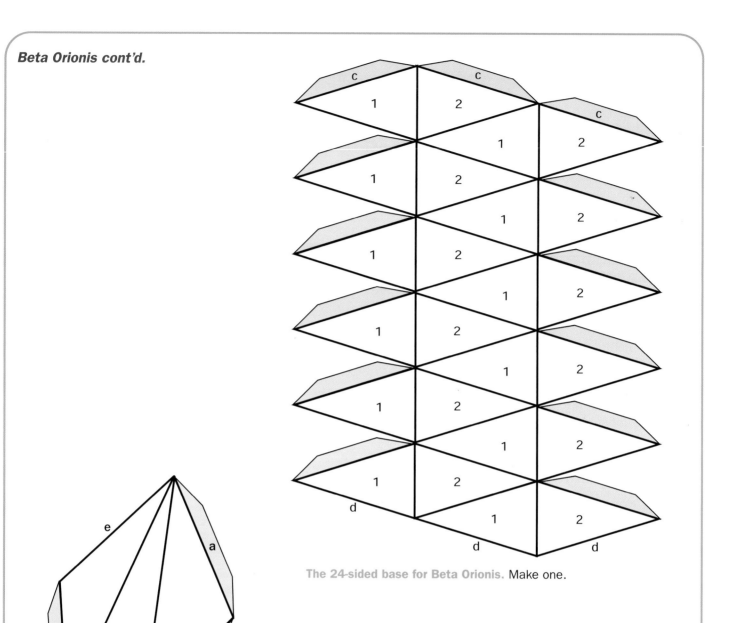

The 24-sided base for Beta Orionis. Make one.

Point 1. Make 12.

Point 2. Make 12.

MARTIAN

Have you ever imagined what Martians are like? This one is about 7" (17 cm) tall, lives in an underground tunnel, and is an expert flying-saucer builder. Fairly stiff paper works best for this project.

1. First make the 3 truncated (shortened) octahedrons: 2 for body parts and one for the head. See the General Instructions for copying patterns. After copying the truncated octahedron pattern, cut out each entire pattern, including the glue flaps. For each octahedron, fold on all lines. Attach the squares to their adjacent hexagons using the 10 green glue flaps. Next glue flap a to edge d, flap b to edge e, and flap c to edge f. Close and complete the base by gluing hexagons H1 and H2 to the yellow y glue flaps.

2. To make the neck, cut out the entire neck pattern, including the glue flaps. Fold on all lines. Attach glue flaps r to the opposite rectangle at edge s.

3. Glue two truncated octahedron parts together on a hexagon face as shown in Photo 1 to make the body. Then glue the neck onto the top hexagon of the body. Let it dry. To add the head, glue the third truncated octahedron on top of the neck using a square face of the octahedron.

4. To make and attach each of the 4 legs, copy and cut out the entire pattern, including the glue flaps. Fold on all lines. Glue flap t to the opposite side of the leg at edge v. Each leg should become a tube with a square opening. Using the remaining glue flaps, glue each leg to the bottom hexagon of the body. Attach the 4 legs in a square pattern, with point i of each leg toward the inside, so that all legs slant outward slightly.

5. Make two of Arm 1 and two of Arm 2. Copy each pattern, and cut out the entire pattern, including the glue flaps. Fold on all lines. Make part 1 of each arm into a tube with a square opening by gluing rectangle p over rectangle q. Make part 2 of each arm into a tube with a square opening by gluing rectangle j over rectangle k. Make part 3 of each arm into a tube with a square opening by gluing rectangle m over rectangle n. Bend each arm at the two joints to the shape you want, and glue into place by putting a dab of glue where the side rectangles of the arm parts overlap after bending. Use each arm's glue flaps to attach the arm to the upper body as shown in the photo.

6. Add eyes, mouth, or even antennae with cut-out paper or a marker.

1. The completed Martian.

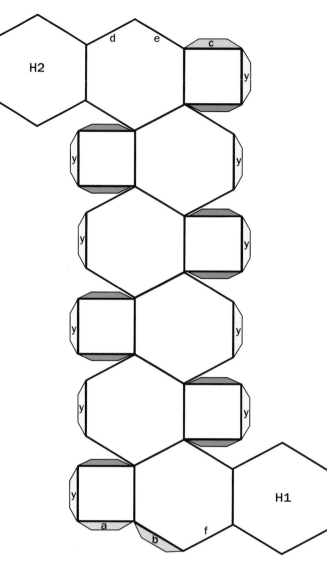

Truncated octahedron for Martian body and head. Make 3.

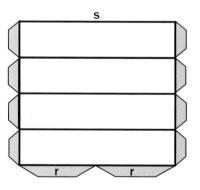

Neck. Make one.

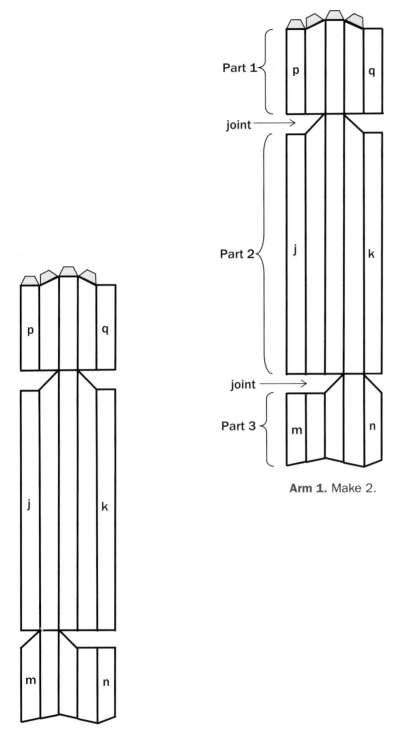

Part 1

joint →

Part 2

joint →

Part 3

p   q

j   k

m   n

Arm 1. Make 2.

p   q

j   k

m   n

Arm 2. Make 2.

point i

t   v

Leg. Make 4.

Make Sirius the scorcher, the brightest star in the Sky. It is also known as the Dog Star.

1. Refer to the General Instructions section of the book for copying patterns. To make the cube base, copy and cut out the entire pattern, including the glue flaps. Fold on all black lines. Glue flap b to the opposite square at edge c. Complete the cube by attaching the top and bottom, using the remaining glue flaps.

2. Make the 14 points: eight of Point 1 and six of Point 2. After copying the patterns, cut out each entire pattern, including the glue flaps. Fold on all lines. Complete each point by gluing flap a to the opposite triangle at edge e.

3. To attach the points to the cube base, place each Point 1 over a corner of the cube, so that it covers a blue area on the pattern. Place each Point 2 on a face of the cube so that it covers an orange area on the pattern.

1. The base.

2. The completed Sirius.

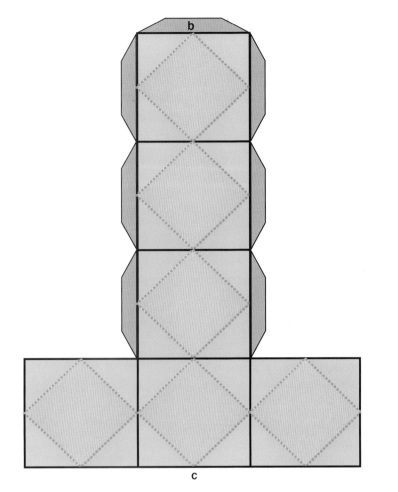

Cube base for Sirius. Make one.

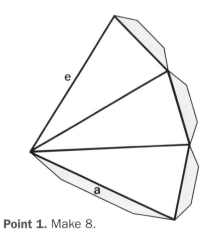

Point 1. Make 8.

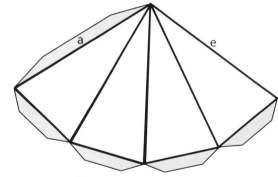

Point 2. Make 6.

Build a Space Probe and send it exploring in outer space. This Space Probe is an octahedron built from 6 small octahedrons. An octahedron is an 8-sided closed solid figure that has equilateral triangles for all 8 faces.

1. Refer to the General Instructions section of the book for copying patterns. First we must construct the 6 small octahedrons, four of Type 1 and two of Type 2. Copy and cut out the entire pattern of each small octahedron, including the glue flaps. Fold on all lines. Glue each flap with an x to the adjacent triangle until the octahedron is complete. The glue flaps labeled with an o should remain on the outside of the figure; they are not used until the next steps.

2. Assemble the four Type 1 small octahedrons into a square arrangement as shown in Photo 1. Use the one o glue flap to attach each octahedron to another, attaching the fourth octahedron to both the third and the first to complete the square.

2. The completed Space Probe.

3. Attach a Type 2 small octahedron on each side of the previously assembled square of four Type 1 octahedrons. Each o glue flap of the Type 2 octahedron attaches to an edge of one of the four Type 1 octahedrons in the square so that one point of the Type 2 octahedron is right at the center of the square.

1. Six small octahedrons for the Space Probe; in center, four Type 1 octahedrons assembled into a square.

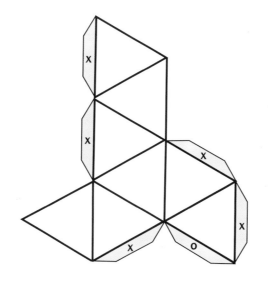

Small octahedron 1 for Space Probe. Make 4.

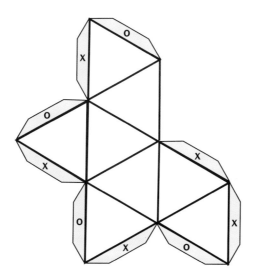

Small octahedron 2. Make 2.

Soleil, or Sun, when translated from French to English, is hot in any language; around 10 000°F at the surface.

1. When choosing paper colors, try all yellow points, all orange points, or a mixture of yellow, orange, and red. A fairly stiff paper is best for the dodecahedron base. A dodecahedron is a solid whose 12 sides are regular pentagons. Refer to the General Instructions section of the book for copying patterns. Copy the base pattern; then cut out the entire pattern, including the glue flaps. Fold on all lines. Glue each flap, one at a time, to the adjacent pentagon.

2. To make the 30 points, after copying the pattern, cut out each entire point pattern, including the glue flaps. Fold on all lines. Assemble each point by attaching glue flap a to edge b (see Photo 1).

3. Attach the points to the base. Each point should be attached over an edge of the base (see Photo 1). The point should be oriented so that each of the corners on a point that has a small sun near it on the pattern is located at the center of a pentagon face on the base (indicated with a small sun on the base pattern). The other two corners of the point should match up with two corners of the base. A base with one point attached is shown in Photo 1.

1. Base with one point attached.

2. The completed Soleil.

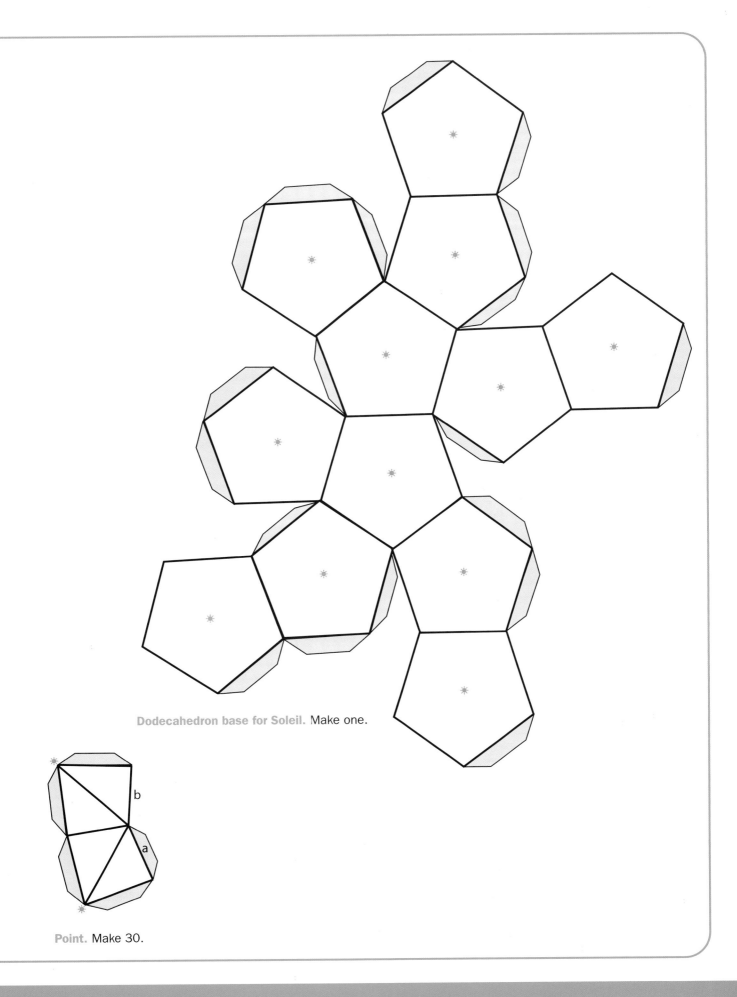

Dodecahedron base for Soleil. Make one.

Point. Make 30.

b

a

PEGASI b

Pegasi b was the first planet discovered to be orbiting another Sunlike star. Pegasi b rotates about its sun (51-Pegasi) every 4 days. The same side of Pegasi b is always facing its sun, so that it is always day on one side of the planet and always night on the other side!

1. Refer to the General Instructions section of the book for copying patterns. Copy the two parts of the pattern to your chosen paper; then cut out each pattern, including the glue flaps. Each gray glue flap should be cut at the edge of the adjacent pentagon (5-sided figure next to it) and remain attached to the edge of the adjacent hexagon (6-sided figure next to it). Fold on all lines. Attach the two parts of the pattern together by gluing flap a on part 1 to flap c on part 2.

2. The planet is then assembled by using the glue flaps to glue each hexagon to the adjacent pentagons. Glue the gray glue flaps first, then the orange o flaps, and last of all the blue b flaps. Be sure to glue the flap on the inside of the adjacent pentagon so that the flaps do not show on the outside of the planet (Photo 1).

1. The completed Pegasi b.

This Pegasi b shape is also known as a truncated icosahedron, because it could be made by cutting off all the corners of an icosahedron (like the Sunburst base).

The pattern can also be used to make a paper soccer ball (Photo 2). Try coloring the pentagons black and the hexagons white.

2. Pegasi b pattern as a soccer ball.

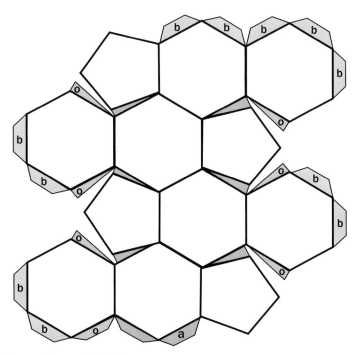

Pegasi b, part 1. Make one.

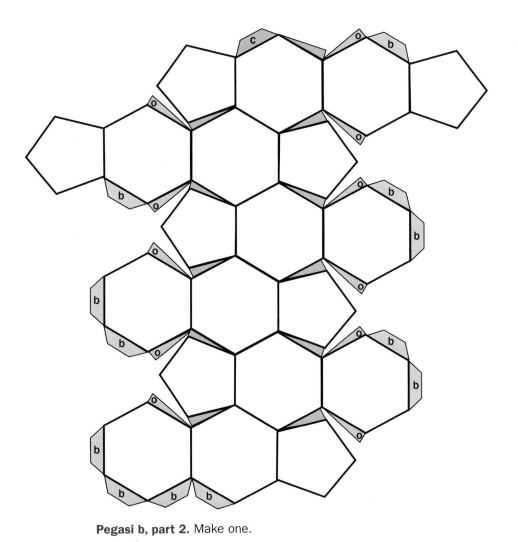

Pegasi b, part 2. Make one.

Meteors criss-cross the paper galaxy. Land one in your town with this Meteorite project.

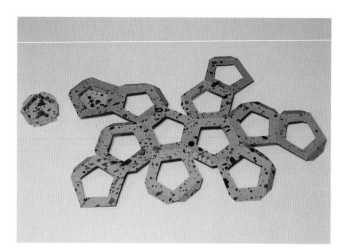

1. Base after folding and cutting and two craters, one attached.

1. Refer to the General Instructions section of the book for copying patterns. You may want to use spattered paper for a rocky appearance. When copying the base pattern, be sure to draw the lines on the side of the paper that will not show on the outside of the meteorite. Copy and cut out the entire base pattern, including the glue flaps. Fold on all black lines and then lay flat again. Next cut out the dashed pentagon from the center of each main pentagon. This can be done with scissors, by first poking a small slit in the center of each pentagon and then cutting on the dashed line. After folding and cutting, the base should look like Photo 1, right side. This base is a dodecahedron, like the base of the Dodec Twinkler.

2. To make the 12 craters for the meteorite, copy the pattern to project paper, and cut out each entire crater pattern, including the glue flaps. Fold on all lines. Glue the rectangular sides of the crater to each other using the triangular glue flaps. The crater should look as shown in Photo 1.

3. Use the remaining 5 rectangular glue flaps on each crater to glue it behind each pentagonal cut-out in the base.

4. To complete the base, use the base's glue flaps to glue each pentagon to the adjacent pentagon until the figure is closed. Be sure the craters are on the inside (Photo 2).

2. The completed Meteorite, with paint-spattered paper.

3. Satellite made with Meteorite pattern.

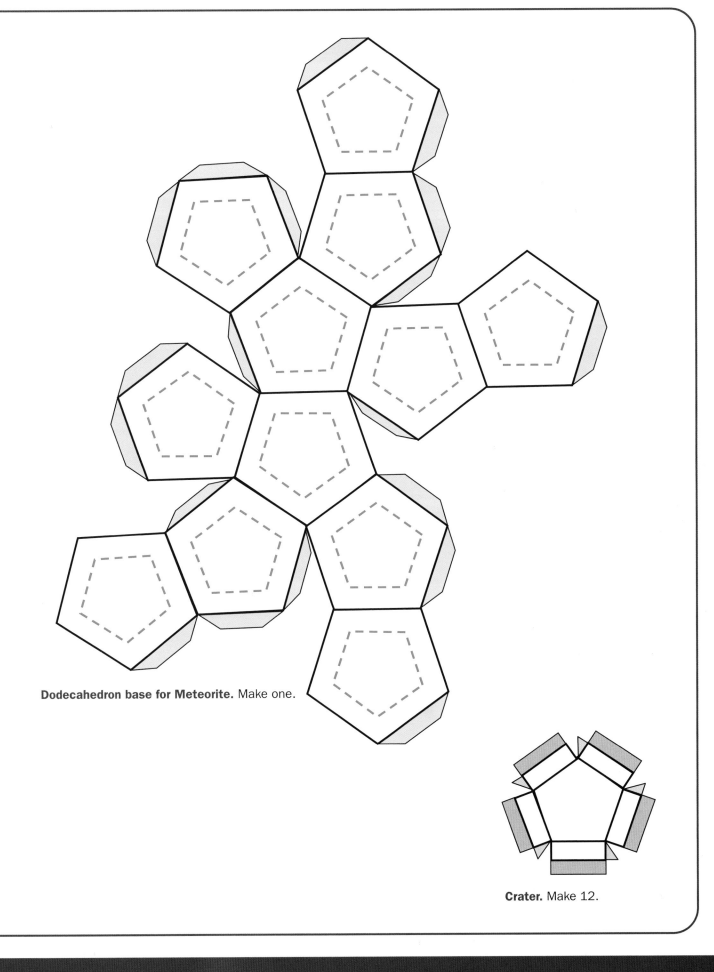

Dodecahedron base for Meteorite. Make one.

Crater. Make 12.

Spin the Spiral Nebula into your night sky.

1. Refer to the General Instructions section of the book for copying patterns. To make 6 double tetrahedrons for the base, copy the double tetrahedron pattern to your chosen paper and cut out each entire pattern, including the glue flaps. Fold on all lines. Glue flap m to the adjacent triangle at edge f; glue flap b to the adjacent triangle at edge g. Complete and close the figure by gluing flap c to edge h and flap d to edge i.

2. To connect the 6 double tetrahedrons together to make the base spiral, first glue 2 of the double tetrahedrons together face to face by attaching points x1, x2, and x3 on the second double tetrahedron to points y1, y2, and y3 on the first double tetrahedron (oriented so that x1 attaches at y1, x2 attaches at y2, etc. (Photo 1, right). Glue the third double tetrahedron to the second by attaching points x1, x2, and x3 on the third to points y1, y2, and y3 on the second. Continue the same way, connecting the fourth to the third, the fifth to the fourth, and the sixth to the fifth. The base spiral will look as shown in Photo 1.

3. Make the 26 points: 24 of Point 1 and two of Point 2. For each point, copy and cut out the entire pattern, including the glue flaps. Fold on all lines. To assemble both kinds of point, attach glue flap a to the opposite triangle at edge e.

4. To attach the points to the base spiral, glue each of Point 1 on a face with an arrow, with the point extending in the direction of the arrow. After attaching all 24 of Point 1, glue a Point 2 on the top and bottom faces of the spiral (see Photos 2 and 3).

1. Six double tetrahedrons; five are already connected to form the base spiral.

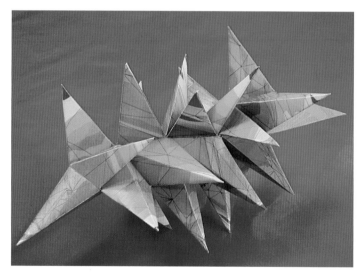

2. A completed Spiral Nebula.

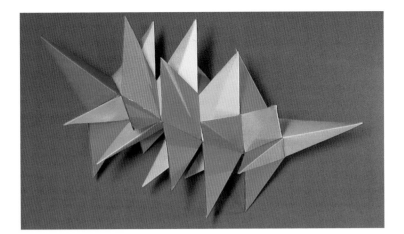

3. A completed Spiral Nebula with points in three colors.

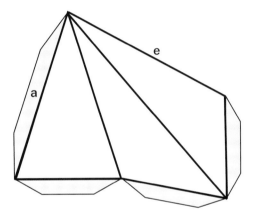

Point 1. Make 24.

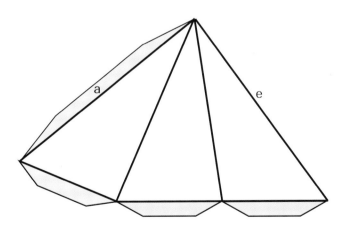

Point 2. Make 2.

Double tetrahedron for base of
Spiral Nebula. Make 6.

4. Another view of the Spiral Nebula.

Do you know that on Venus the Sun rises in the west and sets in the east?
Set your Rising Sun in any direction you like.

1. Refer to the General Instructions section of the book for copying patterns. To make 3 Sun segments, copy the pattern 3 times onto your chosen paper. Cut out each entire pattern, including the glue flaps. Connect the 3 segments together by gluing flaps a on the second segment to edge e on the first segment. Glue flaps a on the third segment to edge e on the second segment.

2. Fold the 3 connected Sun segments. Start by folding on the lines between the trapezoids. (A trapezoid is a 4-sided flat shape that has 2 parallel sides and 2 that are not parallel.) Make mountain folds on the orange lines and valley folds on the blue lines so that the result is a corrugated pattern, with the orange-lined trapezoids becoming the "up" parts of the corrugations and the blue-lined trapezoids becoming the "down" parts of the corrugations. After your folding, the joined Sun segments will make a circular shape. Then glue flaps a on the first segment to edge e on the third segment (Photo 1).

1. Rising Sun segments, connected and folded.

3. To make the points or Sun rays, fold on the lines between the triangles and the trapezoids of the Sun segment, and fold between the triangles and the glue flaps. Make mountain folds at orange lines and valley folds at blue lines. Use the glue flaps to glue each small thin triangle to the adjacent larger triangle.

4. To make and attach the two Sun centers, copy and cut out each entire pattern, including the glue flaps. Fold on the lines between the glue flaps and the circle. Attach the center to the joined segments by gluing the Sun center glue flaps onto each "down" corrugation of the Sun segments (at the center). Let dry. Flip the whole thing over, and glue the other center to the joined segments in the same way on the other side (Photo 2 and 3).

2. The completed Rising Sun.

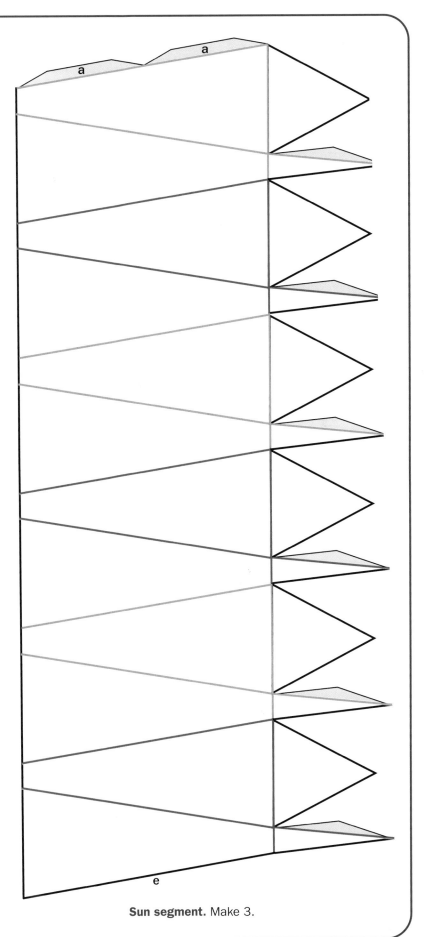

3. Rising Sun, reverse side; for this one the paper was spray-painted before folding.

Sun segment. Make 3.

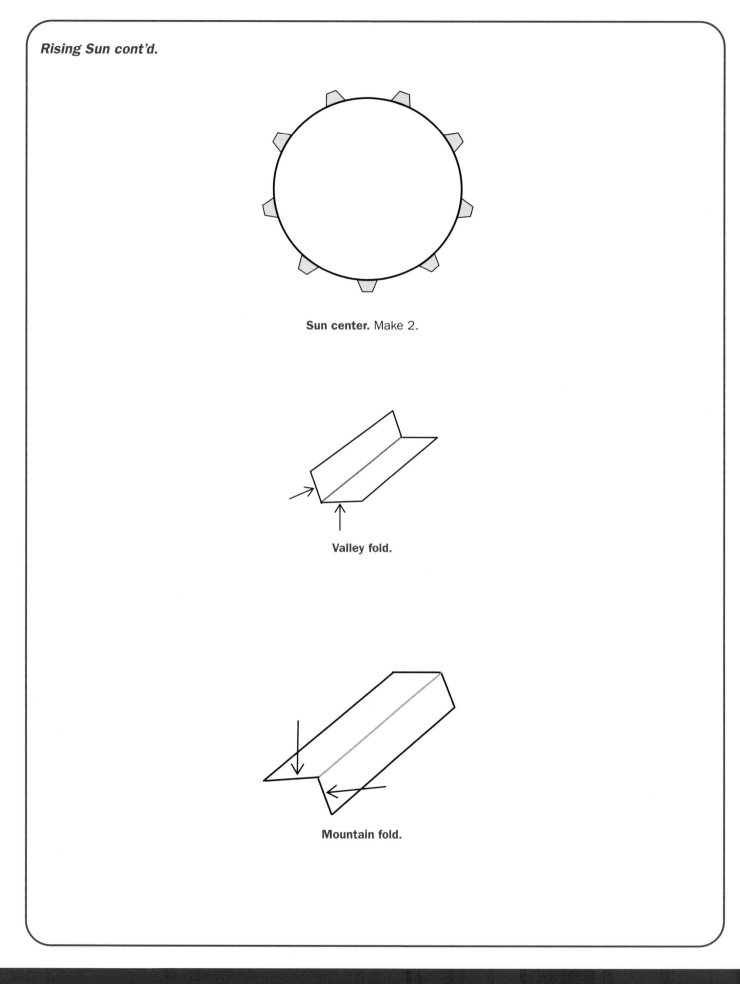

Sun center. Make 2.

Valley fold.

Mountain fold.

Halley's Comet visits the Earth once every 76 years. The next visit will be in 2061. Since that is a long time off, make your own comet now.

1. Base and points 1, 2, 3, and 4 for Comet.

1. Refer to the General Instructions section of the book for copying patterns. To make the icosahedron base (the same base as for the Sunburst), copy and cut out the entire pattern, including the glue flaps. Fold on all lines. Attach each triangle to its neighbor with an unlabeled glue flap; then close the base by gluing flaps c to edges d. Photo 1 shows the base and 4 points.

2. Make the 16 points for the tail of the comet: one of Point 1; five of Point 2; five of Point 3; and five of Point 4. Make them all one color or vary the colors. After copying the point patterns, cut out each pattern, including the glue flaps. Fold on all lines. Complete each point by gluing glue flap a to the opposite edge e (Photo 1).

3. Attach the points to the base using the remaining point glue flaps. Attach Point 1 directly over the point on the base labeled p; each glue flap on Point 1 should attach to one triangle of the base so that the point completely covers the blue area. This Point 1 will be the center of the comet tail. Next glue five Point 2's around Point 1. Each Point 2 should cover the orange area on a face of the base. Next glue each of the five Point 3's to a face of the base labeled T. Glue each of the five Point 4's to a face of the base labeled U. All points should be oriented to point toward the tail of the comet. The 5 unlabeled faces of the base remain uncovered and form the head of the comet (Photos 2 and 3).

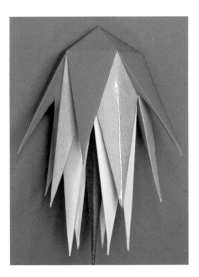

2. A completed Comet, with points in several colors.

3. A completed Comet, all in one color.

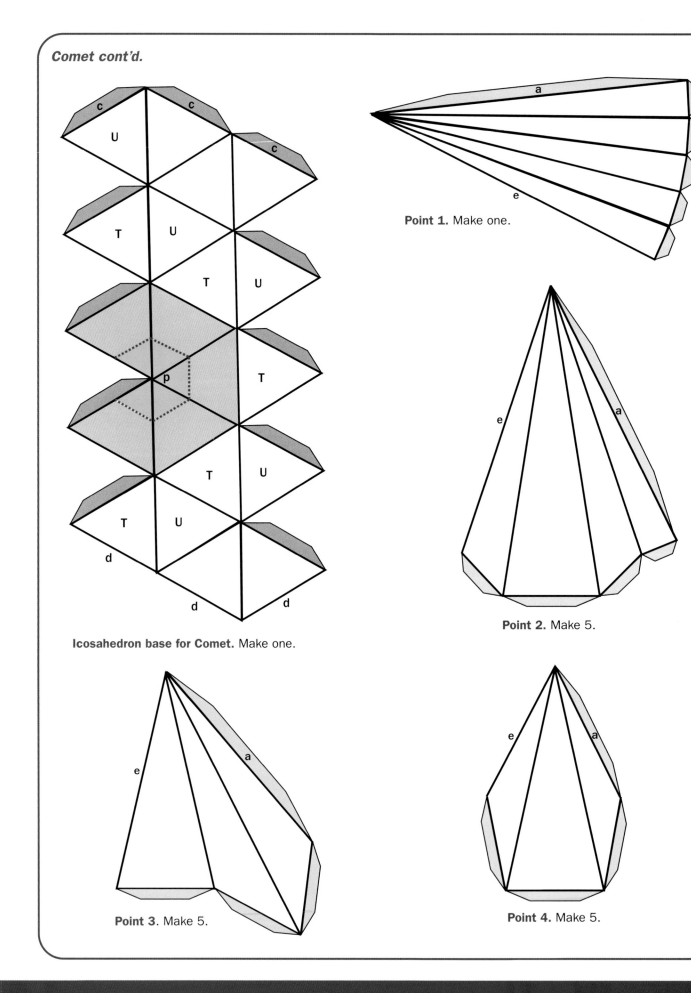

Point 1. Make one.

Icosahedron base for Comet. Make one.

Point 2. Make 5.

Point 3. Make 5.

Point 4. Make 5.

Omega Centauri is a globular star cluster in the Centaurus constellation. This project is also a star cluster with 12 stars in one.

1. Refer to the General Instructions section of the book for copying patterns. To make the dodecahedron base, copy parts 1, 2, 3, and 4 of the base onto your chosen paper and cut them out, including the glue flaps. Connect the 4 parts of the base pattern together by gluing flap f on part 1 to flap g on part 4; flap h on part 2 to flap j on part 4; and flap k on part 3 to flap m on part 4. Fold on all lines. Complete the base by gluing each of the remaining glue flaps to its adjacent pentagon until the figure is closed. Be sure to attach the flaps on the inside of the adjacent pentagon, because parts of the base will show, even after attaching the points. Photo 1 shows the completed base with one point attached.

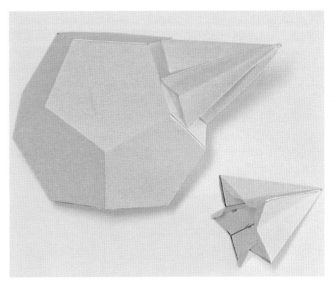

1. Omega Centauri base with two points, one attached.

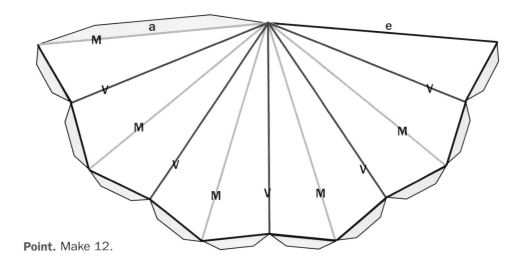

Point. Make 12.

2. To make the 12 star-shaped points, copy and cut out each entire point pattern, including the glue flaps. Fold the V-labeled lines inward like a valley; fold the M-labeled lines outward like a mountain. Complete each point by attaching glue flap a to edge e. Completed points should look as shown in Photo 1, right.

3. Attach one point on each face of the base, using the remaining glue flaps on that point. The point should be attached so that it covers the star-shaped area on each pentagon face of the base. As shown in Photo 2, the corners of the base will remain visible and make an interesting small point between each of the star points.

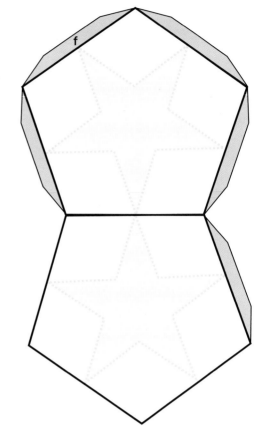

Omega Centauri base part 1. Make one.

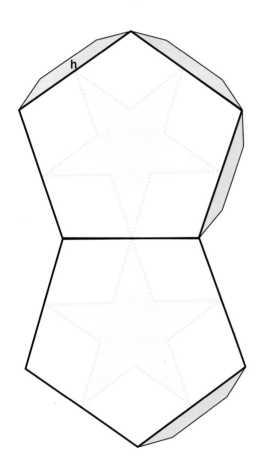

Base part 2. Make one.

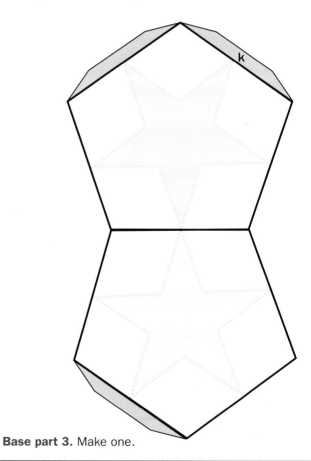

Base part 3. Make one.

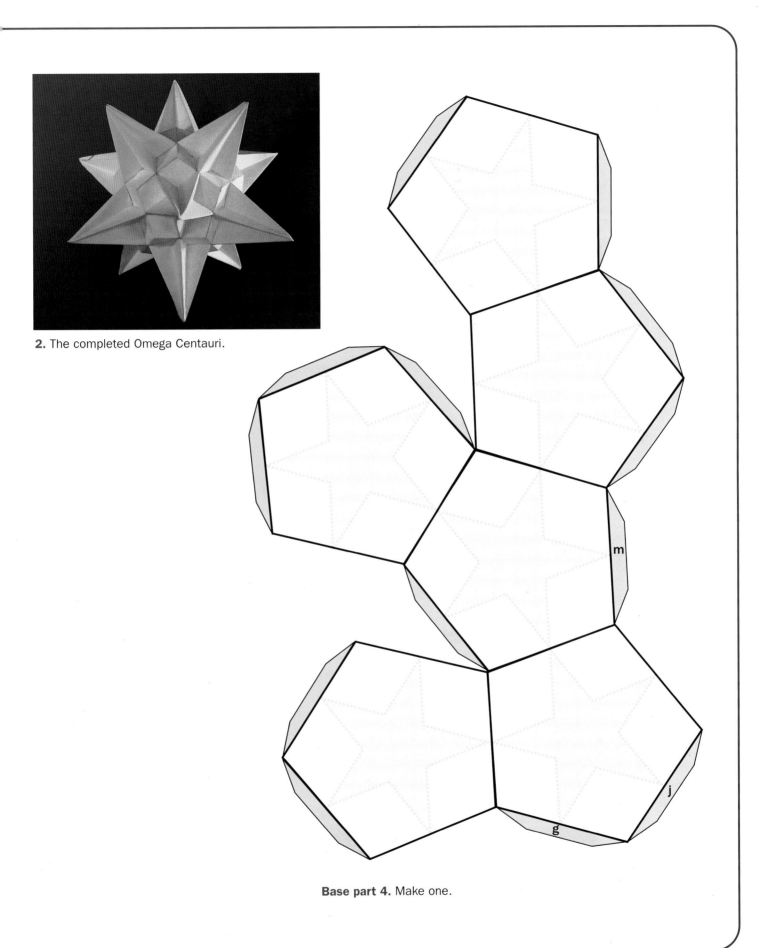

2. The completed Omega Centauri.

m

j

g

Base part 4. Make one.

Take this Rocket Ship to the Moon, stop for lunch, and then continue to Mars.

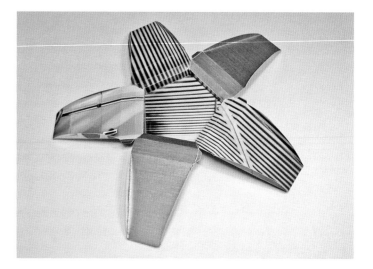

1. The base, just after gluing the y glue flaps of base part 2.

1. Refer to the General Instructions section of the book for copying patterns, and copy the patterns to your chosen papers. To make the base, you need one copy of base part 1 and five of base part 2. For base part 1, just cut out the pentagon; no folding is required. For base part 2, cut out each entire pattern, including the glue flaps. Fold on all lines. Attach the five base part 2's to base part 1 by gluing each flap c to one edge of base part 1. Next fold the lower rectangles on the five base part 2's (with the x glue flaps) and glue these rectangles to each other, using the x glue flaps. Next fold the thin trapezoids on the base part 2's (with the y glue flaps), and glue these trapezoids to each other, using the y glue flaps. The base should now look like Photo 1. Now turn the base over. Fold the next rectangles (with the z glue flaps) on the base part 2's upwards, and glue these rectangles to each other, using the z glue flaps. Finally, connect the large trapezoids of the base part 2's together by gluing the fins of the adjacent parts to each other, face to face, so that the fins stick out from the sides of the base (Photo 2, right).

2. To make the rocket body, cut out the entire pattern from your chosen paper, including the glue flaps. Fold on all lines. Glue the two glue flaps q to opposite edge p.

3. To make the rocket nose cone, copy and cut out the entire pattern, including the glue flaps. Fold on all lines. Glue flap a to opposite edge e. Photo 2 shows a nose cone.

4. Make the flames: one of flame 1 and five each of flame 2 and 3. For all 11 flames, start by copying and cutting out each entire pattern, including the glue flaps, and folding on all lines. For flame 1, connect the adjacent trapezoids using the o glue flaps. For flames 2 and 3, connect flap b to edge f, and connect flap a to edge e.

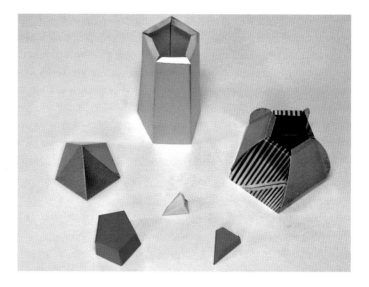

2. Back row, left to right: nose cone, body, base. Front row: flame 1, flame 3, flame 2.

5. Use the remaining glue flaps on flames 1, 2, and 3 to attach the flames to the similarly numbered areas on base part 1 (Photo 3).

6. To attach the nose and the base to the body of the rocket, glue flaps n on the body to glue flaps d on the base; fold flaps inside so that they do not show after attaching the two pieces. In a similar way, attach the nose cone glue flaps to glue flaps m on the body.

3. Base with flames.

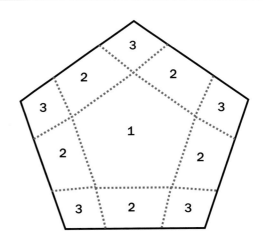

Rocket Ship base, part 1. Make one.

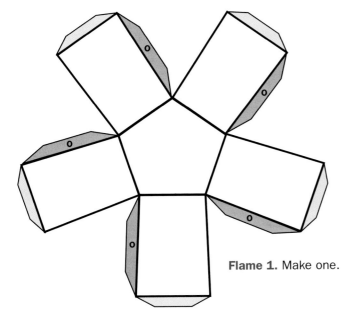

Flame 1. Make one.

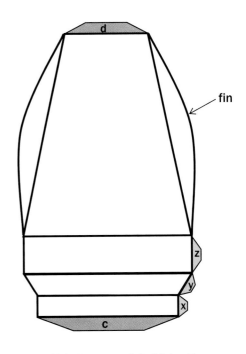

fin

Rocket Ship base, part 2. Make 5.

4. The completed Rocket Ship.

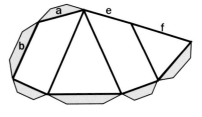

Flame 2. Make 5.

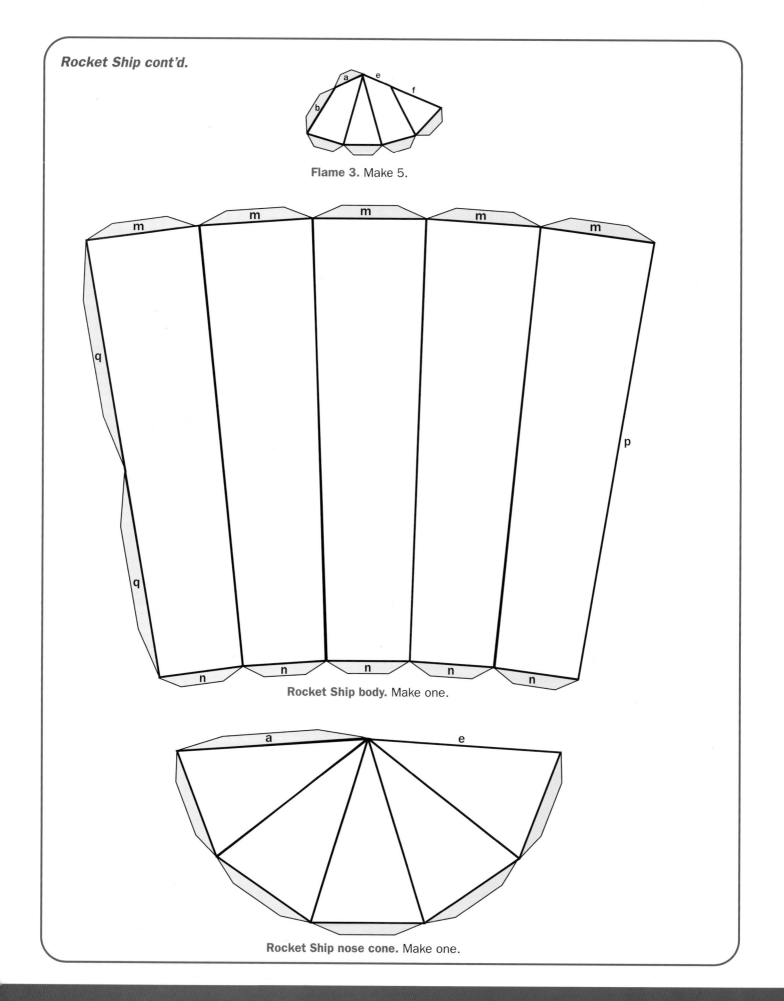

Flame 3. Make 5.

Rocket Ship body. Make one.

Rocket Ship nose cone. Make one.

Add the exploding Supernova to your star collection.

1. Refer to the General Instructions section of the book for copying patterns. To make the tetrahedron base, copy the pattern to your chosen paper and cut out the entire pattern, including the glue flaps. Fold on all lines. Glue flap f to edge g. Close and complete the tetrahedron using the remaining two glue flaps.

2. Make 4 of the intermediate projections. After copying the pattern, cut out each entire pattern, including the glue flaps. Fold on all black lines. Glue flap h to edge i. Complete each projection by attaching each edge d to its adjacent glue flap c.

3. To attach the intermediate projections to the base tetrahedron, use the 3 remaining glue flaps on each intermediate projection to glue it to one of the faces of the tetrahedron (see Photo 1).

4. Make sixteen of Point 1 and twelve of Point 2. After copying the patterns, cut out each entire pattern, including the glue flaps. Fold on all lines. On each point, glue flap a to edge e.

5. Glue four Point 1's to each intermediate projection. First use the glue flaps on one point to attach it on the center of the triangular face of the projection, over the yellow-shaded area. Then attach one Point 1 over each corner of the projection; one to cover the orange-shaded area, one to cover the blue-shaded area, and one to cover the green-shaded area.

6. Attach 3 Point 2's to each intermediate projection. Use the glue flaps on each point to glue it just behind the Point 1's, covering a purple-shaded area.

1. Tetrahedron base with intermediate projections attached. Made of a transparent plastic sheet.

2. The completed Supernova.

3. Another view of the Supernova.

Supernova cont'd.

The example shown has clear plastic sheeting (used in offices for overhead projections) for the base and the intermediate projections. With this type of material, it may be necessary to use craft glue rather than normal white glue.

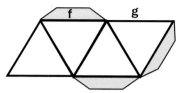

Tetrahedron base for the Supernova. Make one.

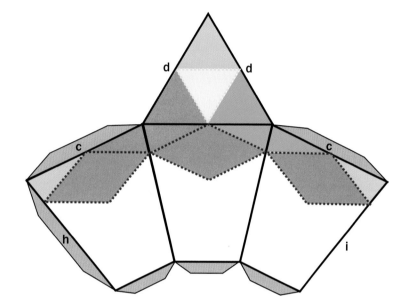

Intermediate projection. Make 4.

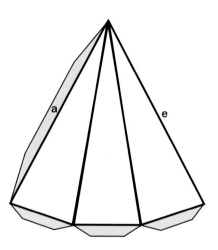

Point 1. Make 16.

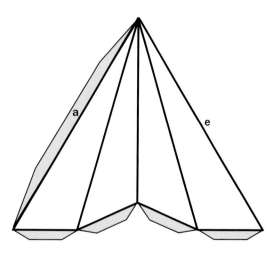

Point 2. Make 12.

QUASAR

Quasars are starlike objects, extremely distant from Earth, that emit large quantities of radio waves and light.

1. Refer to the General Instructions section of the book for copying patterns. To make the cube base, copy the pattern to your chosen paper and cut out the entire pattern, including the glue flaps. (It is not necessary to include the 4-pointed star shape on each square in your pattern. Those shapes are gluing guides for the points.) Fold on all lines. Glue flap c to edge d. Complete the cube base by gluing on the top and bottom of the cube, using the remaining glue flaps.

2. Make 6 of Point 1. For each, cut out the entire pattern, including the glue flaps. Fold on all lines. Glue flap a to the opposite edge e.

3. Glue the six Point 1's to the base. One is attached to each face of the cube, using the triangular glue flaps on the point. When attaching, push in the sides of the point at the orange circles, so that the sides curve inward as shown in Photo 1. The point should about cover the 4-pointed star shape shaded in blue dots on the pattern. Hold the point in its curved shape while the glue dries.

4. Make 12 of Point 2. For each, cut out the entire pattern, including the glue flaps. Fold on all lines. Glue flap a to opposite edge e.

5. Glue the 12 Point 2's to the base. One point is attached over each edge of the base cube between the Point 1's, using the Point 2's triangular glue flaps. When attaching, squeeze the point into a football shape so it completely fills the area between the Point 1's. Hold each point in its curved shape while the glue dries. Photos 2 and 3 show two views of the completed Quasar.

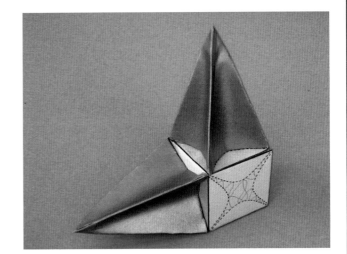

1. Cube base of Quasar with two of Point 1 attached. The blue area indicates where point should be glued.

2. The completed Quasar.

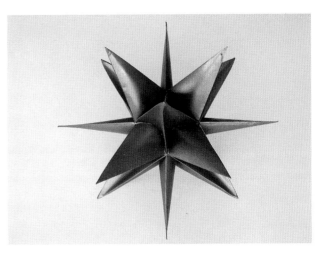

3. Another view of the completed Quasar.

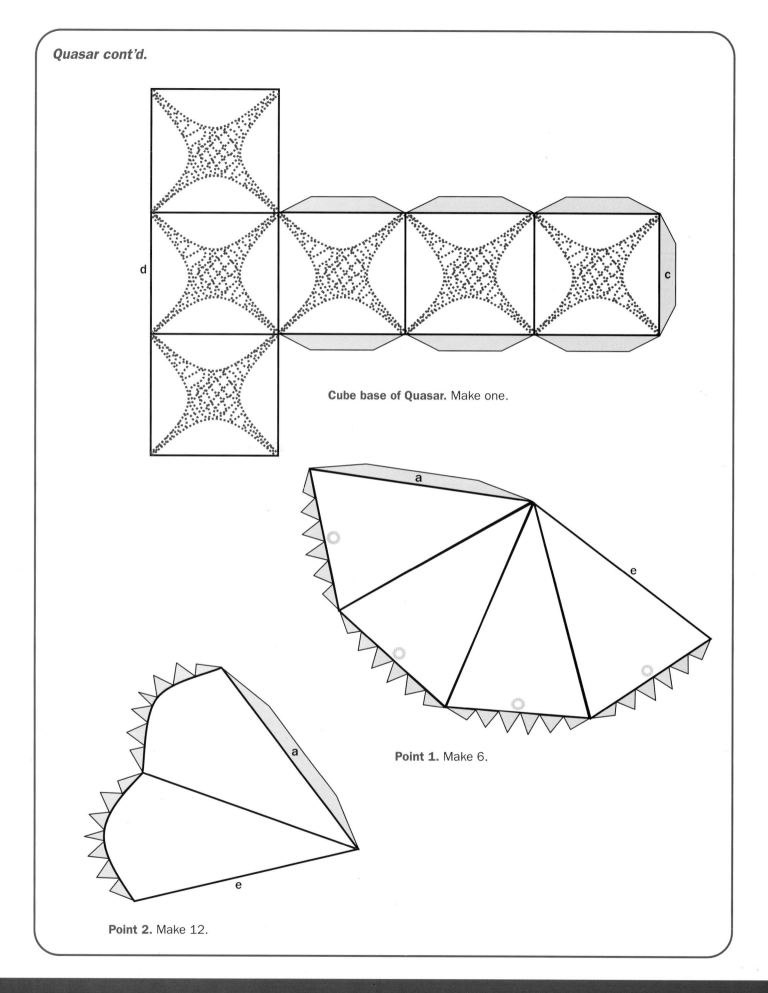

Cube base of Quasar. Make one.

Point 1. Make 6.

Point 2. Make 12.

Faint but beautiful, Epsilon Eridani is the ninth-closest star to our own Sun.

1. Refer to the General Instructions section of the book for copying patterns. Make the base. A fairly stiff paper, like card stock, will work best for this base. Part of the base remains visible, so choose a paper color that looks good with the paper selected for the points. Copy two of the base half-patterns to your chosen paper, and cut out each entire pattern, including the glue flaps. Connect the base halves together by gluing together the a glue flap on the first base half to the a glue flap on the second base half so that the two halves connected look as shown in Diagram 1. Next, fold on all lines where two circles join and between the circles and the glue flaps. Glue each of the small circles of the base to the adjacent large circles using the 10 orange o glue flaps. Next glue the 3 g green glue flaps on the first base half to the 3 green g glue flaps on the second base half. Finally, complete the base by gluing the 2 circles labeled C1 onto the blue b glue flaps. The completed base should look as shown in Photo 1.

2. Make 8 of Point 1 and 6 of Point 2. After copying the patterns to project paper, cut out each entire pattern, including the glue flaps. Fold on the lines between the glue flaps and the point. Roll each point into a cone. The orange circle marks the point that will be the center and point of the cone. Roll into a cone until point w reaches point x, and then continue to roll into a smaller, pointier cone until point w reaches point y. The cone should now be two layers thick at all points, with the glue flaps going around the full circumference of the lower layer. Glue into this shape by lifting up the edge (edge with blue line in pattern) and gluing under this edge.

1. The completed base.

3. Attach the 14 points to the base: Glue each Point 1 to a large circle face of the base, and glue each Point 2 to a small circle face of the base, using the point's glue flaps. Each point should be centered on the circle face; a thin ring of each base circle face will remain visible around each point, as shown in the photo to the right.

2. The completed Epsilon Eridani.

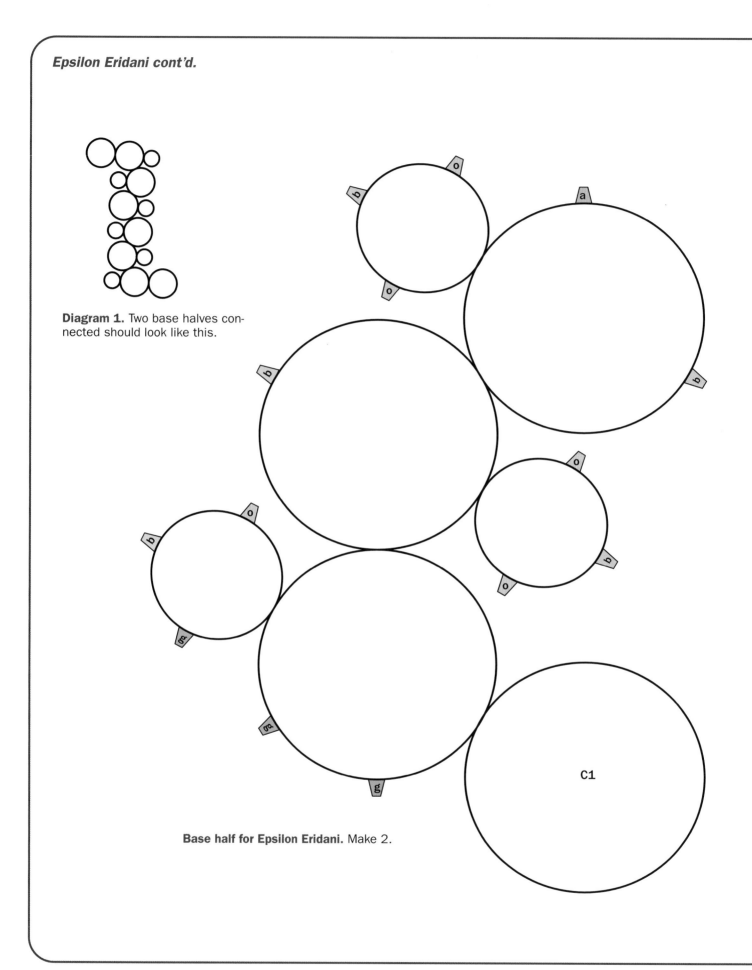

Diagram 1. Two base halves connected should look like this.

Base half for Epsilon Eridani. Make 2.

C1

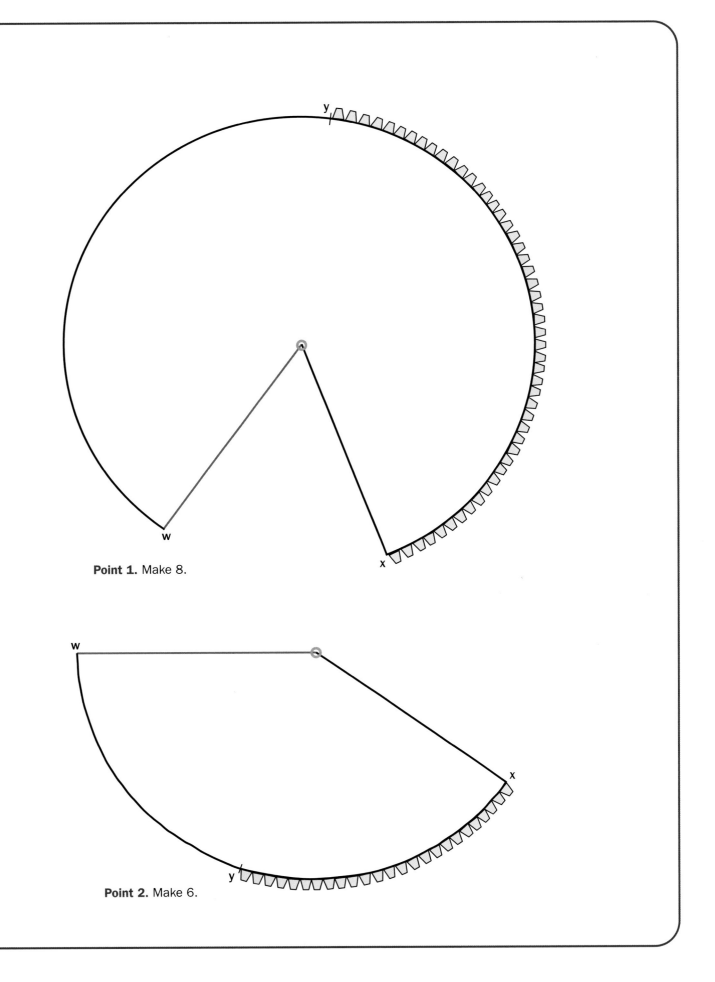

Point 1. Make 8.

Point 2. Make 6.

A Protostar is a new star being formed. As it spins, you can still see through it in places.

1. Refer to the General Instructions section of the book for copying patterns. Make the base, which is an irregular cubeoctahedron. A cubeoctahedron is a polyhedron with 8 tri-angle faces and 6 tetragon (4-sided) faces. After copying the pattern to your chosen paper, cut out the entire pattern, including the glue flaps. Fold on all lines. Then flatten out again and cut out the center areas on 12 of the faces by cutting on the green dashed lines. This can be done with scissors by first poking a hole through the center of the cut-out area and then cutting. Refold. Complete the base by attaching each unlabeled glue flap to the adjacent face of the base. Lastly, glue flaps f and g to edges h and i. Photo 1 shows the completed base.

2. Make the 3 patterns for the sides of the points; one each of Point Side 1, 2, and 3.

3. Make the 14 points. There are 7 different-shaped faces on the base pattern, which are labeled p, q, r, s, t, u, and v. You will make a different point to go with each of these faces. Face t of the base, for instance, has sides labeled 2, 1, and 2; so you draw the whole point for that face using side pattern 2, side pattern 1, and then a side pattern 2 again, as shown in Example 1 (page 67). Add glue flaps as shown in Example 1 after you have drawn the whole point. Cut out the entire pattern, including the glue flaps. Fold on the lines between the 3 sides and between the sides and the glue flaps. Flatten out again. Make the interior cut-outs on the whole point by cutting on the green dashed lines (see Photo 2). Refold and com-plete the point by gluing the 3 glue flaps on edge a to the opposite edge e. Face u has sides labeled 2, 3, 1, and 2, so you draw the point for face u using side patterns 2, 3, 1, and 2 (again) as shown in Example 2. In the same way, make a point for each face of the base cubeoc-tahedron. You will need two points for each of shapes p, q, r, s, t, u, and v.

1. The completed base.

2. Left: point with cut-outs ready for refolding and gluing. Right: a completed point.

4. Glue the points to the base using the remaining point glue flaps, each point over its corresponding face.

3. The completed Protostar.

4. Protostar, another view.

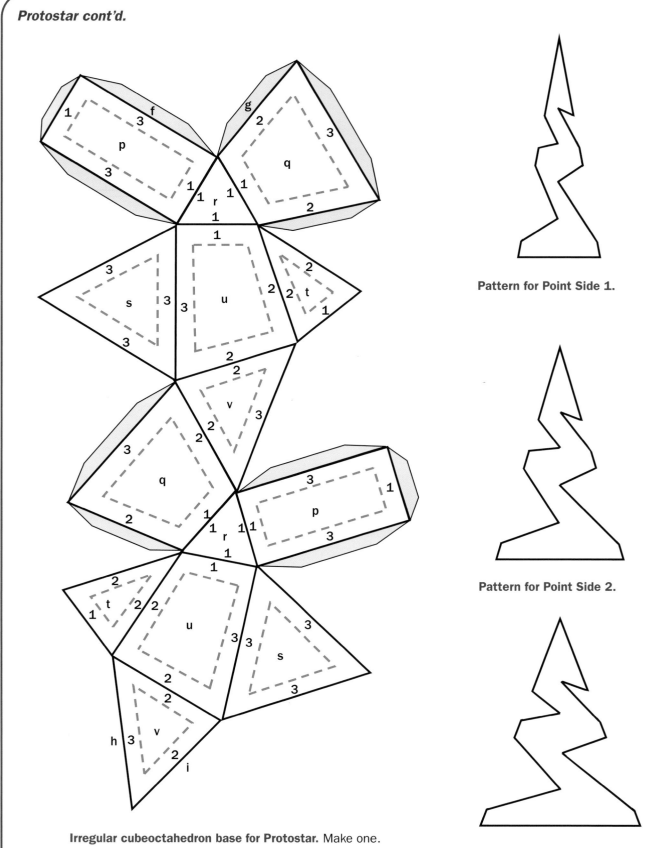

Irregular cubeoctahedron base for Protostar. Make one.

Pattern for Point Side 1.

Pattern for Point Side 2.

Pattern for Point Side 3.

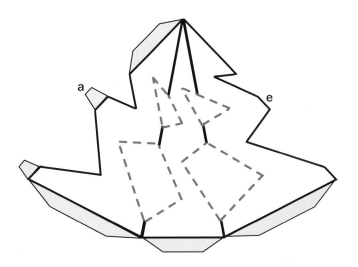

Example 1. Point pattern for face t, using Point Side 2, 1, and 2 patterns. Glue flaps have been added.

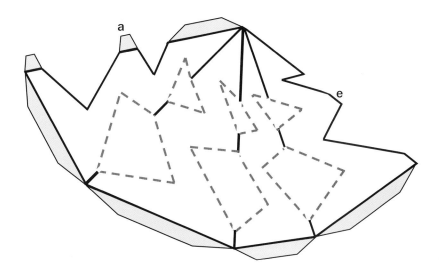

Example 2. Point pattern for face u, using Point Side patterns 2, 3, 1, and 2. Glue flaps have been added.

Have you ever wondered what it would be like to live out in space on a space station? Make a model of your dream space station.

1. Refer to the General Instructions section of the book for copying patterns. To make 6 of branch 1, copy the pattern to your chosen project paper, and cut out each entire pattern, including the glue flaps. Detach the glue flaps from the small trapezoids and leave the glue flaps attached to the long trapezoids by cutting on the red lines. Fold on all lines. Make the branch into a long octagonal prism by gluing flap a to edge e. Glue down the 4 small trapezoids, 2 at each end, to the triangular glue flaps. Complete the branch by gluing the rectangle at each end of the branch to the remaining glue flaps. A completed branch 1 is shown in Photo 1.

2. Make 5 of branch 2. Copy and cut out each entire pattern from project paper, including the glue flaps. Fold on all lines. Make into a long octagonal prism by gluing flap a to edge e. A completed branch 2 is shown in Photo 1 on the left.

3. To connect the branches, use the glue flaps on the end of a branch 2 to connect it to the side of a branch 1. Next connect a branch 1 to the other end of the branch 2. Continue by adding a branch 2, and then a branch 1 at the end of the newly added branch 2, until all branches are attached. Branches can be attached in any arrangement to make your dream space station design.

To make a larger space station, just make additional branch 1's and branch 2's, an equal number of each, and add anywhere. There is plenty of space out there!

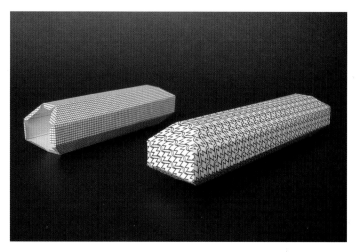

1. Branch 2 (left) and branch 1 (right).

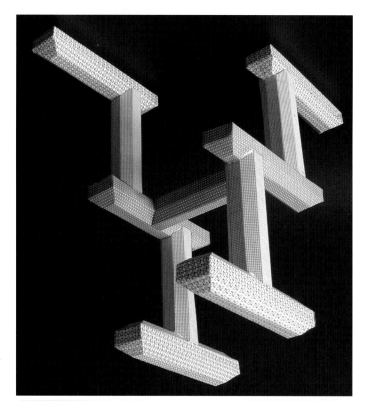

2. The completed Space Station, built from envelope paper that was turned inside out.

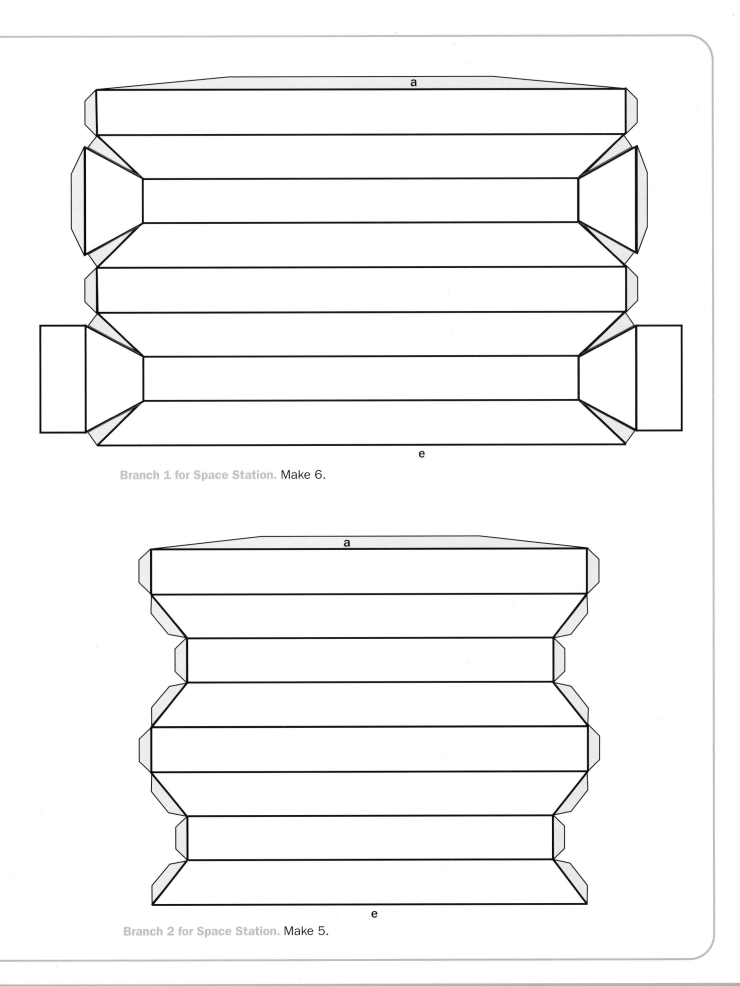

a

e

Branch 1 for Space Station. Make 6.

a

e

Branch 2 for Space Station. Make 5.

The T Tauri star is irregular—sometimes bright, sometimes dim, in no particular pattern.

1. Refer to the General Instructions section of the book for copying patterns. To make the tetrahedron base, copy the pattern to your chosen project paper and cut out the entire pattern, including the glue flaps. Fold on all lines. Glue flap a to edge e. Close and complete the tetrahedron base, using the remaining glue flaps.

2. Make 4 of Point 1. For each, copy and cut out the entire pattern, including the glue flaps. Fold on all lines. Glue flap c to edge d and flap f to edge g. Next glue flap h to edge i and flap j to edge k.

3. Attach the four Point 1's to the base by gluing a Point 1 to each face of the tetrahedron base using the three b glue flaps (see Photo 1).

4. Make 6 of Point 2. For each, copy and cut out the entire pattern, including the glue flaps. Fold on all lines. Glue flap s to edge t and flap u to edge v. Next glue flap m to edge n, glue flap o to edge p, and glue flap q to edge r.

5. Attach the six Point 2's to the previously constructed base, which has the Point 1's already attached. Attach a Point 2 between each of the Point 1's, using the 4 glue flaps labeled w. Orient points so that the red diamonds on Point 2 are adjacent to the red diamonds on Point 1 and the blue asterisks on Point 2 are adjacent to the blue asterisks on Point 1.

1. Four of Point 1 attached to the base; at right, a completed Point 2.

2. The completed T Tauri.

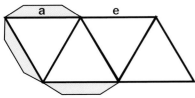

Tetrahedron base for T Tauri. Make one.

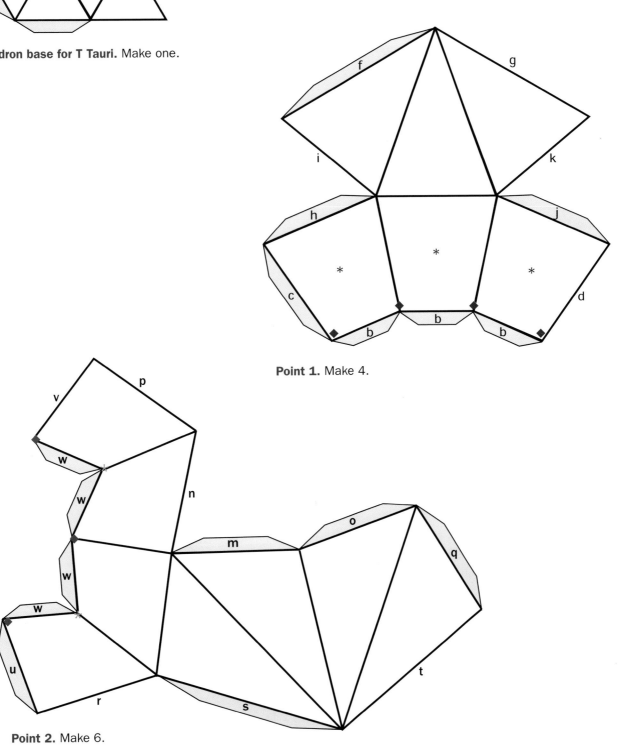

Point 1. Make 4.

Point 2. Make 6.

Have you ever wondered whether there could be a world on a speck of dust and even a smaller world on a speck of dust in that world? Make this world within a world within a world. This project is made of 3 icosahedrons, one inside the other.

1. Refer to the General Instructions section of the book for copying patterns. Fairly stiff paper works best for this project. To make the small icosahedron, copy the pattern to project paper, and cut out the entire pattern, including the glue flaps. Fold on all solid lines. Flatten out again. Cut out the inside dashed green triangles on all 20 faces by first poking a small starter slit in the center of each triangle with scissors and then cutting. Refold on solid lines. Use a needle to poke a small hole through the pattern near one corner (such as the point marked with a red circle). Use the needle to pull a thread, knotted at one end, through the hole until the knot is pulled against what will become the inside of the icosahedron. Glue each triangle to the adjacent triangle using the unlabeled glue flaps. Complete and close the pattern by attaching the c glue flaps to the d edges. See Photo 1 for the completed small icosahedron. Don't cut off the extra thread or needle.

2. To make the middle icosahedron, copy and cut out the entire pattern, including the glue flaps, fold on all solid lines, flatten out again, and cut out the inside dashed green triangles. Use a needle to poke a small hole through the pattern near one corner (such as the point marked with a red circle). Glue 6 of the unlabeled glue flaps to adjacent edges. Then place the small icosahedron inside the partially completed middle icosahedron so that the holes for the thread line up. Use a needle to pull the thread from the small icosahedron through the hole in the middle icosahedron. Close the middle icosahedron, using the

1. The small icosahedron.

remaining glue flaps. Fix the small icosahedron in the center of the middle icosahedron by placing a small dab of glue where the thread comes through the hole.

3. To make the large icosahedron, start by making 5 copies onto your project paper of the large icosahedron pattern part shown. Glue flap a on one part to edge b on the next part until all 5 parts are connected to make a full icosahedron pattern (It should look the same as the small and middle icosahedrons, but bigger.) Repeat the steps described above for making the middle icosahedron, but this time place the middle plus small icosahedron inside the partially completed large icosahedron before gluing the last 5 flaps in place. Glue the thread in place.

Display hanging on the thread.

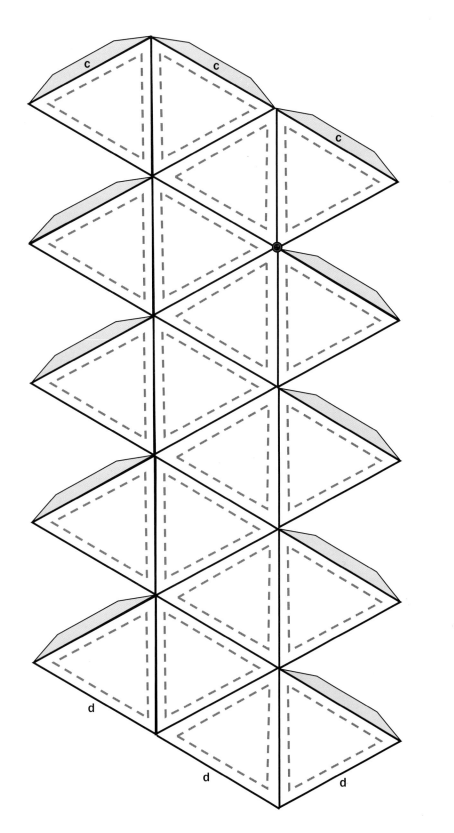

Middle icosahedron for World Within. Make one.

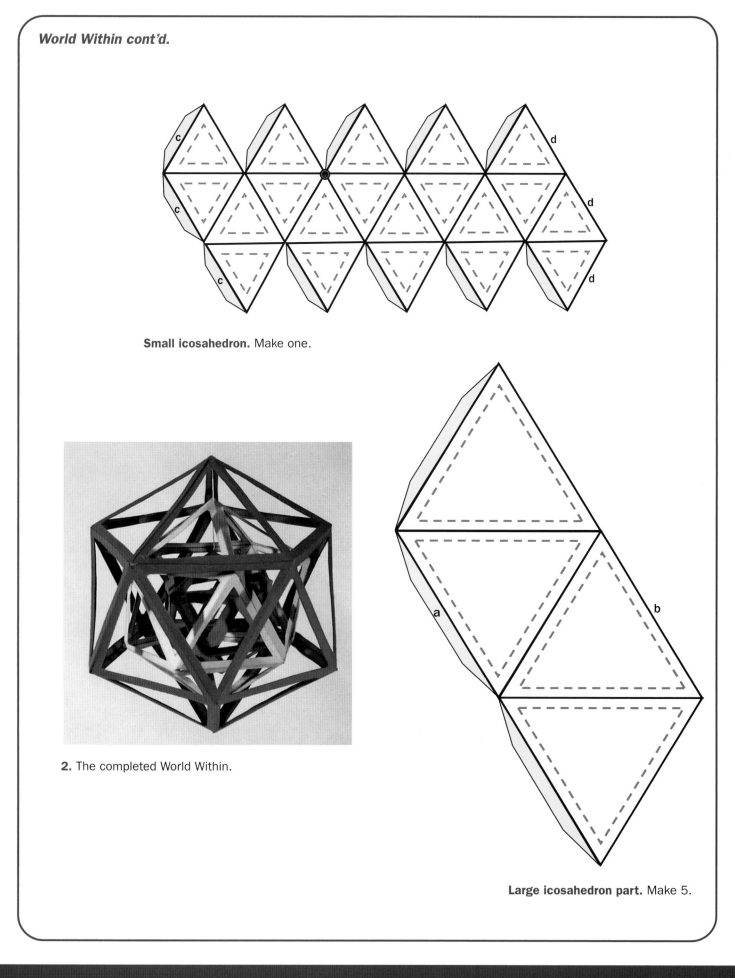

Small icosahedron. Make one.

2. The completed World Within.

Large icosahedron part. Make 5.

Beware the Black Hole; nothing can escape its gravity.

1. Refer to the General Instructions section of the book for copying patterns. Make the 32 points. Make 12 of Point 1 and 20 of Point 2. After copying the patterns to project paper, cut out each entire pattern, including the glue flaps. Fold on all lines. Fold so that the front side of the paper (the side which you want to show) is on the inside of each point. Fold glue flap a toward the front side of the paper, and fold all other glue flaps toward the back side. Complete the point by attaching glue flap a to the opposite edge e. The glue flap should be attached on the outside of the point so that it will not show.

2. Attach the points together with the points oriented toward the center of the Black Hole. The inside surface of the point should be showing (see Photo 1). The 5-sided points (Point 1) and 6-sided points (Point 2) are arranged in the same way as the pentagons and the hexagons on the Pegasi b project. There are five 6-sided points surrounding each 5-sided point. Glue the points together with the remaining glue flaps, flap to flap, with the flaps folded down between the points so they do not show after the points are connected. See photos.

1. Two points connected.

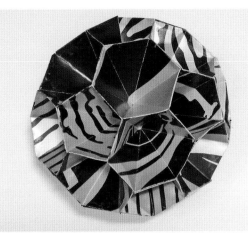

2. The completed Black Hole.

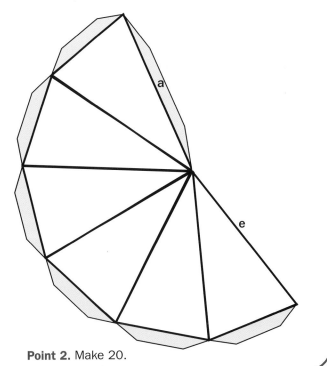

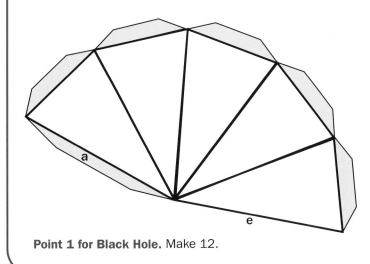

Point 1 for Black Hole. Make 12.

Point 2. Make 20.

Pollux is a large star that is about 40 light-years from Earth. This Pollux is mysterious, with 14 peaks surrounded by dark valleys.

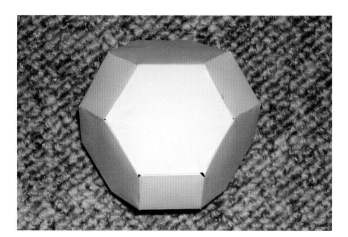

1. The truncated octahedron.

1. Refer to the General Instructions section of the book for copying patterns. Make the truncated octahedron base. It is called a truncated octahedron, because it is an octahedron with the points cut off. After copying the base pattern to project paper, cut out the entire pattern, including the glue flaps. Fold on all lines. Attach the squares to the adjacent hexagons using the 10 orange o glue flaps. Next glue flaps r, s, and t to edges u, v, and w. Close and complete the base by attaching hexagons H1 and H2 to the blue b glue flaps. Photo 1 shows a completed truncated octahedron base.

2. Make the 14 points: 8 hexagonal points and 6 square points. After copying the patterns to project paper, cut out each entire pattern, including the glue flaps. Fold on all black lines first. Next carefully fold each red line segment so that the red line is the peak of a mountain fold. Then carefully fold each blue line segment so that the blue line is the bottom of a valley. While bringing glue flaps a, c, and d around to meet edges e, f, and g, push the top of the point downward, so that the red lines become a ring of mountain folds and the blue lines become a ring of valley folds. A cross-section of a point with its mountains and valleys is shown with the point patterns. Glue flaps d, c, and a to edges g, f, and e. The above instructions are for both the hexagonal and square points.

3. Attach the points to the base: Glue a hexagonal point to each hexagonal face of the base, and glue a square point to each square face of the base, using the remaining glue flaps on each point. Photos 2 and 3 are two views of the completed Pollux.

2. The completed Pollux.

3. Another view of the completed Pollux.

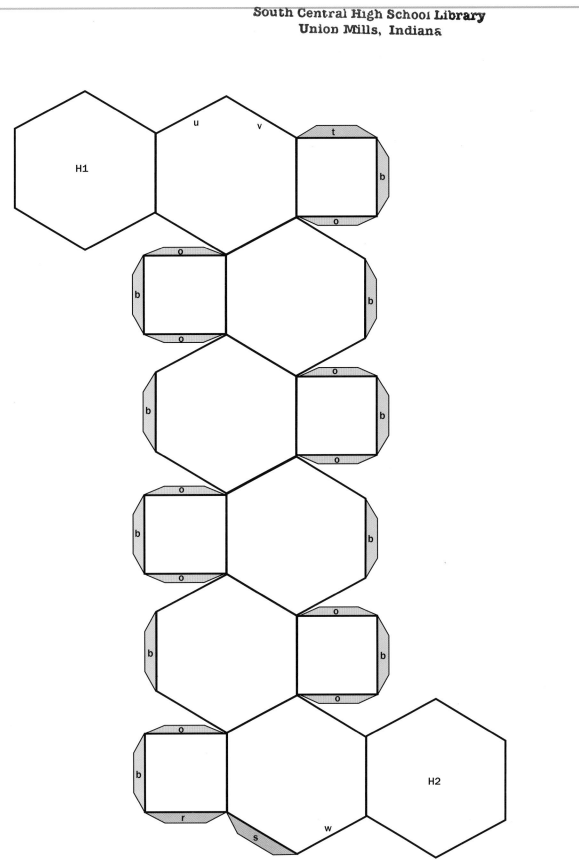

The truncated octahedron base for Pollux. Make one.

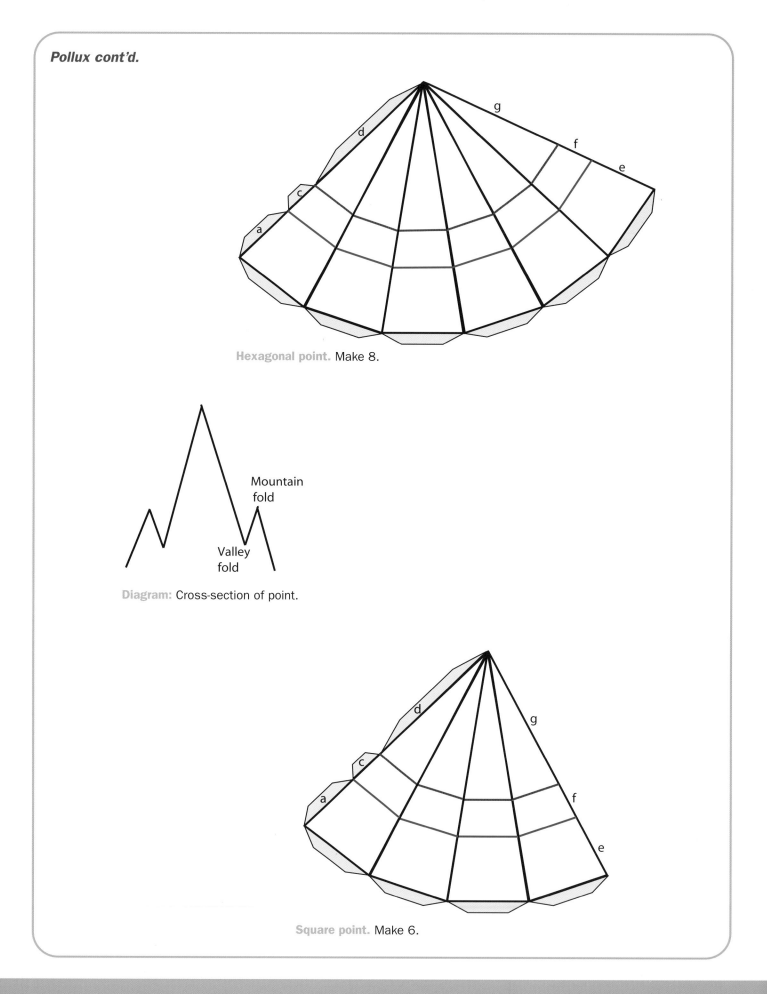

Hexagonal point. Make 8.

Mountain fold

Valley fold

Diagram: Cross-section of point.

Square point. Make 6.

TOROID STAR

What does a geometry whiz call a doughnut? You guessed it—a toroid. This one is a hexagon in one dimension and a pentagon in the other.

1. Refer to the General Instructions section of the book for copying patterns. For the Toroid base, copy 6 of the base segment (part) pattern to project paper and cut out each entire pattern, including the glue flaps. Fold on all lines. Glue flap p to opposite edge q on all 6 segments. Next glue flaps c, d, e, f, and g on the second segment to edges h, i, j, k, and l on the first segment. Glue flaps c, d, e, f, and g on the third segment to edges h, i, j, k, and l on the second part. Continue gluing segments together around the Toroid; close and complete it by connecting the sixth segment to both the fifth segment and the first segment. Photo 1 shows the base and 3 points.

2. Make the points: 12 of Point 1, 6 of Point 2, 6 of Point 3, and 6 of Point 4. For each point, copy and then cut out the entire pattern, including the glue flaps. Fold on all lines. Glue each flap a to the opposite edge e on that point.

3. With the remaining glue flaps on each Point 1, attach it to one of the faces of the Toroid base that is shaded yellow on the pattern. Six will point in one direction and six in the other. In the example shown in Photo 2, each ring of Point 1's has alternating yellow and orange points.

4. With the remaining glue flaps on each Point 2, attach one to every other face of the Toroid that is shaded orange on the pattern, skipping one orange face in between. Do this on both sides of the Toroid.

5. With the remaining glue flaps on each Point 3, attach each Point 3 to a face of the Toroid that is shaded orange on the pattern (the faces that are not already covered by Point 2's).

6. With the remaining glue flaps on each Point 4, attach each over an edge of the Toroid, as shown on the diagram with the Point 4 pattern. These points will cover the faces of the Toroid that are shaded blue on the base pattern. Each Point 4 will cover half of a blue face on one Toroid base segment and half of a blue face on the adjacent Toroid base segment, with the point's edge located at the dotted line on the Toroid base.

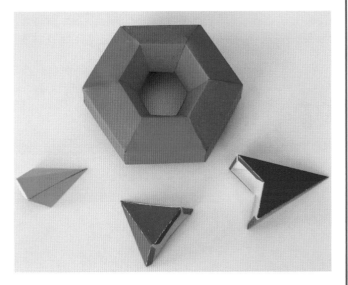

1. Toroid base and (left to right) points 1, 2, and 4.

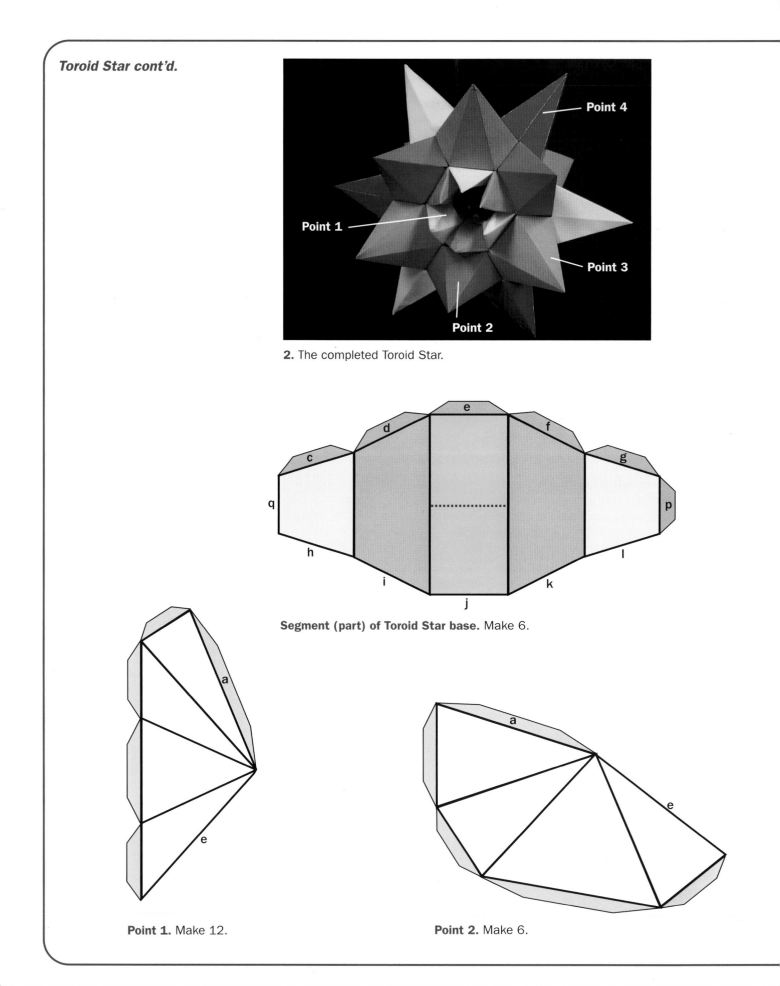

2. The completed Toroid Star.

Segment (part) of Toroid Star base. Make 6.

Point 1. Make 12.

Point 2. Make 6.

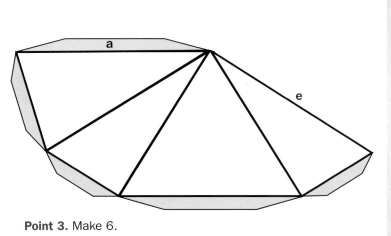

Point 3. Make 6.

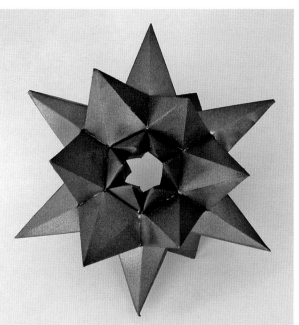

3. Another Toroid Star, painted after it was assembled.

Point 4. Make 6.

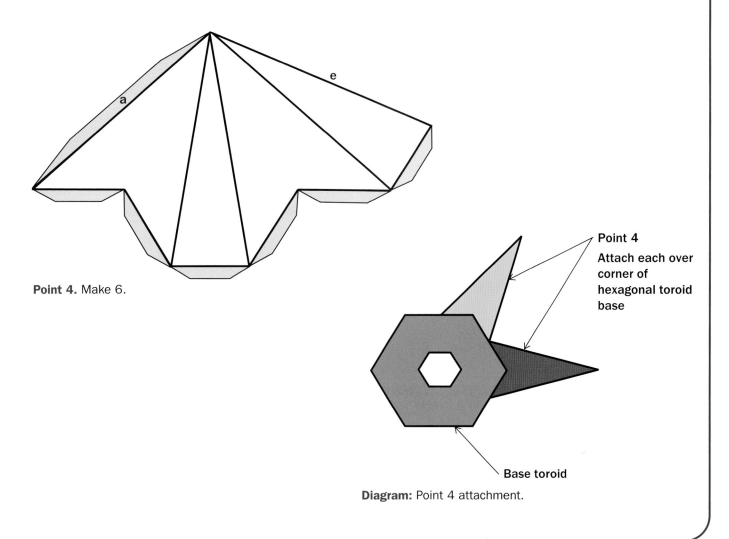

Point 4
Attach each over corner of hexagonal toroid base

Base toroid

Diagram: Point 4 attachment.

Are aliens friendly? Depends how you draw them.

1. Refer to the General Instructions section of the book for copying patterns. Make the toroid base using the pattern and instructions provided for the Toroid Star project.

2. Make 6 flames. For each flame, copy the pattern to project paper, and then cut out the entire pattern, including the glue flaps. Fold on all lines. Glue flap a to opposite edge e.

3. Using the remaining glue flaps on the flame, attach it to one of the faces of the toroid base that is shaded yellow on the pattern, but only attach flames to the 6 yellow-shaded faces on one side of the base (see Photo 1). This side will be the bottom of the Spaceship.

4. To make the 6 wings, copy the pattern to project paper and cut out each entire pattern, including the glue flaps. For each wing, fold on all lines. Glue flap g to opposite edge h and at the same time glue flap c to adjacent edge d.

5. Attach the 6 wings to the toroid base: Using the remaining glue flaps on each wing, attach it to one of the faces of the toroid base that is shaded blue on the pattern. Photo 1 shows the wings attached.

6. Make the capsule. A clear plastic acetate sheet, such as is used for office overhead projections, will work well. After copying the capsule pattern, cut out the entire pattern, including the glue flaps. Fold on all lines. Glue flap m to opposite edge n. Attach the hexagon top of the capsule to the 5 glue flaps marked s.

7. Make aliens, control consoles, and whatever else you want in your Spaceship. Glue them to the toroid base so that they will fit inside the capsule.

8. Glue the capsule to the toroid base using the remaining glue flaps on the capsule (Photo 2).

1. Alien Spaceship, bottom view, with flames and wings showing.

2. Alien Spaceship, side view.

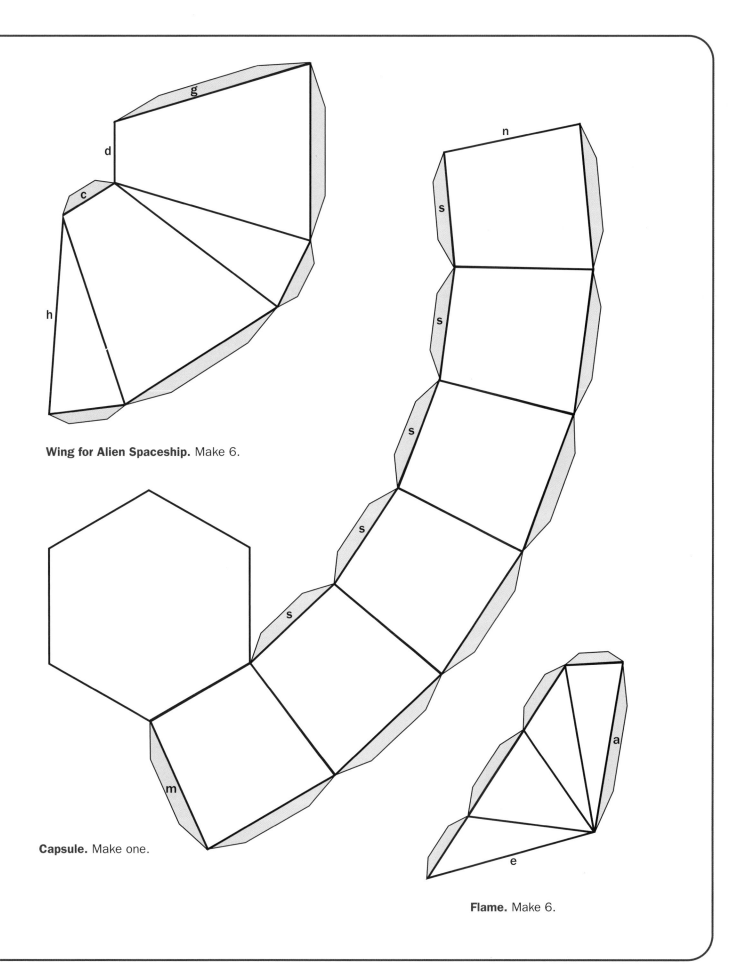

Wing for Alien Spaceship. Make 6.

Capsule. Make one.

Flame. Make 6.

SEDNA

Sedna is the newest planet in the solar system. It is about 2 000 000 000 miles beyond Pluto; about 6 000 000 000 miles from Earth. It would take 40 years to get there on the space shuttle.

1. A fairly stiff paper like card stock is required for this project. Refer to the General Instructions section of the book for copying patterns. Each point will be a different color from the adjacent points if you use 3 colors of paper as follows: Make all 6 of Point 1 from one color (all salmon-colored in example) and make 4 of Point 2 from each of the other two colors (4 blue and 4 purple in example). You need to make a total of 6 of Point 1 and 8 of Point 2. Copy the patterns to project paper and cut out each entire pattern, including the glue flap. Fold on all solid lines. Attach glue flap a to edge e. To complete each point, fold upwards on blue lines (valley fold) so that completed points look like the ones in Photo 1.

2. Connect the points together to form Sedna. Points are connected by gluing each upward-folded tip to an upward-folded tip on another point. Each tip of a Point 1 is attached to a tip of a Point 2. On Point 2's, half the tips are attached to Point 1 tips and half the tips are attached to Point 2 tips, alternating as you go around the six Point 2 tips: Point 1 tip, Point 2 tip, Point 1 tip, Point 2 tip, Point 1 tip, point 2 tip. The best way to understand the pattern in which the points are attached to each other is to look at the truncated octahedron base of the Pollux project. Place a Point 1 in the position of each square face and a Point 2 in the position of each hexagon face with the tips coming together at each edge of the truncated octahedron. One way to start is to attach 4 points together, two of Point 1 and two of Point 2, as shown in Photo 2. Next attach 2 adjacent tips from a new Point 2 (blue) to the two tips labeled d on Photo 2.

3. Continue by attaching two adjacent tips of another new Point 2 (purple) to the two tips labeled f in Photo 2. Do the same on the two tips labeled h and the two tips labeled g in the photo. Next glue the tip of a new Point 1 to the tip labeled i and the tip of another new Point 1 to the tip labeled j. Attach two opposite tips of each of these new Point 1's to the adjacent Point 2 tips. Your construction should now look as shown in Photo 3. Next attach a new Point 2 tip to the remaining tip on each of these newly added Point 1's, which are labeled k in Photo 3. Connect together the opposite tips of these newly added Point 2's. Lastly add two Point 1's in the remaining gaps and attach all tips.

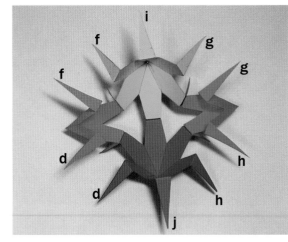

1. A completed Point 2 (left) and Point 1.

2. Four points joined, two of Point 1 (salmon) and two of Point 2 (1 blue, 1 purple).

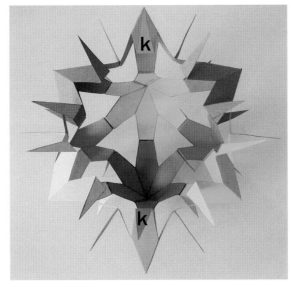

3. Ten points joined.

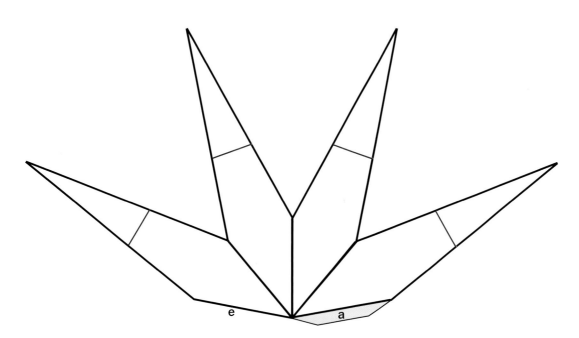

Point 1, Sedna. Make 6.

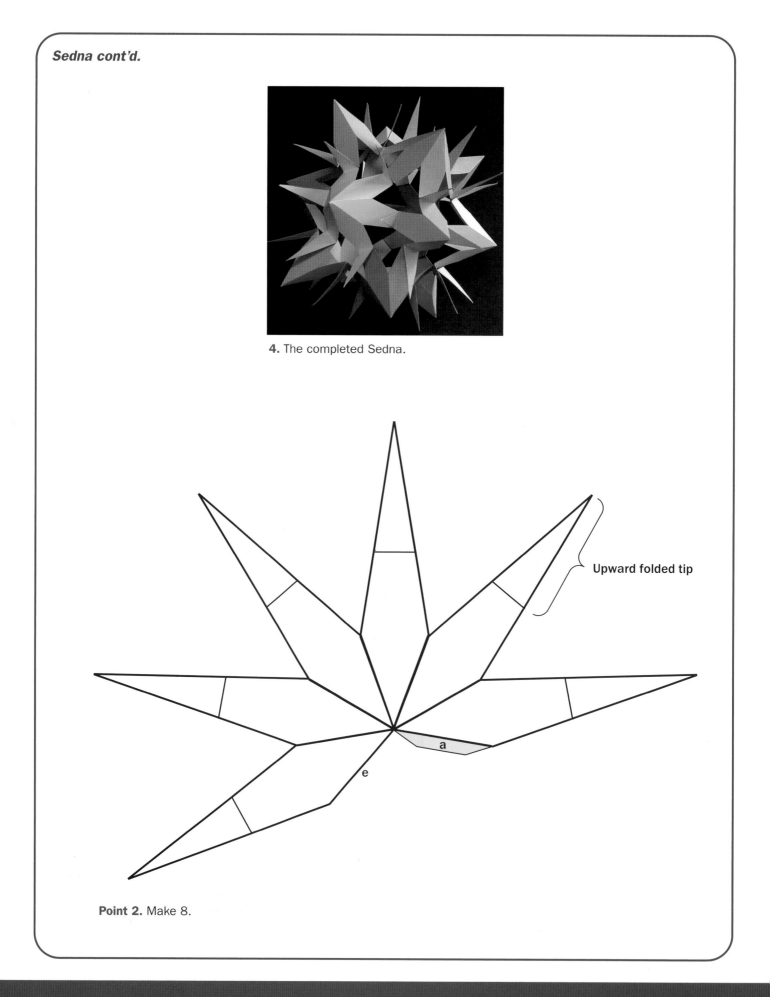

4. The completed Sedna.

Upward folded tip

a

e

Point 2. Make 8.

Discover this menacing star on a dark and scary Cimmerian Night.

1. Refer to the General Instructions section of the book for copying patterns. First, make the base, a rhombicubeoctahedron (a cube with both the corners and the edges cut off). It has 26 faces and 24 vertices (corners). After copying the base pattern to project paper, cut out the entire pattern, including the glue flaps. Fold on all lines. Assemble the base by attaching each numbered glue flap to the edge with the same number. Start with green flaps 12, 13, 17, 18, 19, 20, 21, and 22; continue around until the base is completed and closed. See completed base in Photo 1.

2. To make the 24 points, copy the points to project paper and cut out each entire pattern, including the glue flaps. Fold on all lines. Complete the point by attaching glue flap a to edge e.

3. Each point is attached over one corner (vertex) of the base. As you can see on Photo 1, each corner of the base is surrounded by 3 square faces and one triangle face. Glue flap t on the point should be attached to the triangle face, and 2 glue flaps are attached to each square face, as shown in the diagram with the base pattern.

1. The completed base.

2. The completed Cimmerian Night. Points were made from used envelopes, turned inside out.

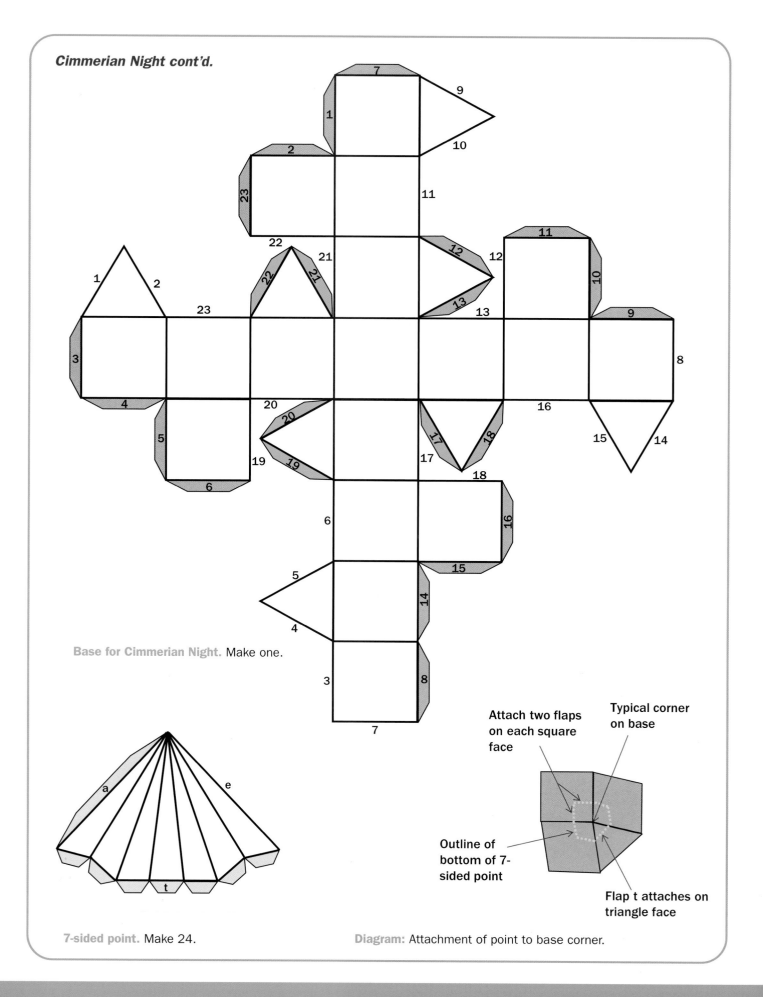

Base for Cimmerian Night. Make one.

7-sided point. Make 24.

Attach two flaps on each square face

Typical corner on base

Outline of bottom of 7-sided point

Flap t attaches on triangle face

Diagram: Attachment of point to base corner.

Light up your holiday with this Four July Sky Star.

1. Refer to the General Instructions section of the book for copying patterns. Choose a paper for this star that looks good on both sides. A paper that is one color on the front and another color on the back works especially well. A metallic foil-type paper, like the kind shown in the photos, may require craft glue instead of normal white glue. To make the base, copy the truncated pyramid base pattern to your chosen paper and cut out the entire base pattern, including the glue flaps. Fold on all lines. Glue all orange o flaps to the adjacent edges of the base. Complete and close the base by gluing the octagon face onto the remaining 7 glue flaps. This base is a square pyramid with the corners cut off--a truncated pyramid. See the completed base in Photo 1.

2. Make the 22 points: two of Point 1, four of Point 2, twelve of Point 3, and four of Point 4. After copying the required number of patterns to project paper, cut out each entire point pattern, including the glue flaps. Fold on all lines. Fold the points so that the outside of the point is the opposite color of the base and the upper side of the glue flaps (the side which is not glued) is the same color as the base.

3. To attach the points to the base, glue each lettered glue flap of a point (c, d, e, f, g, h) over the corresponding-lettered area on the base. The bottom edges of the point should match and align with the corresponding edges on the base.

To hang the Four July Sky Star, attach a thread with a dab of glue to the center of the square face on the base.

1. The truncated pyramid base (left) and a Point 1.

2. The completed Four July Sky Star. In this photo the outer side of the point's glue flaps are the same color as the outside of the base.

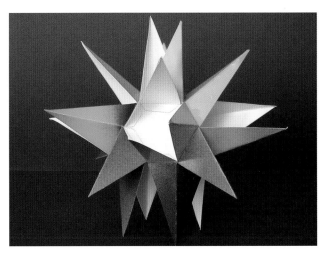

3. Four July Sky Star in green and white paper.

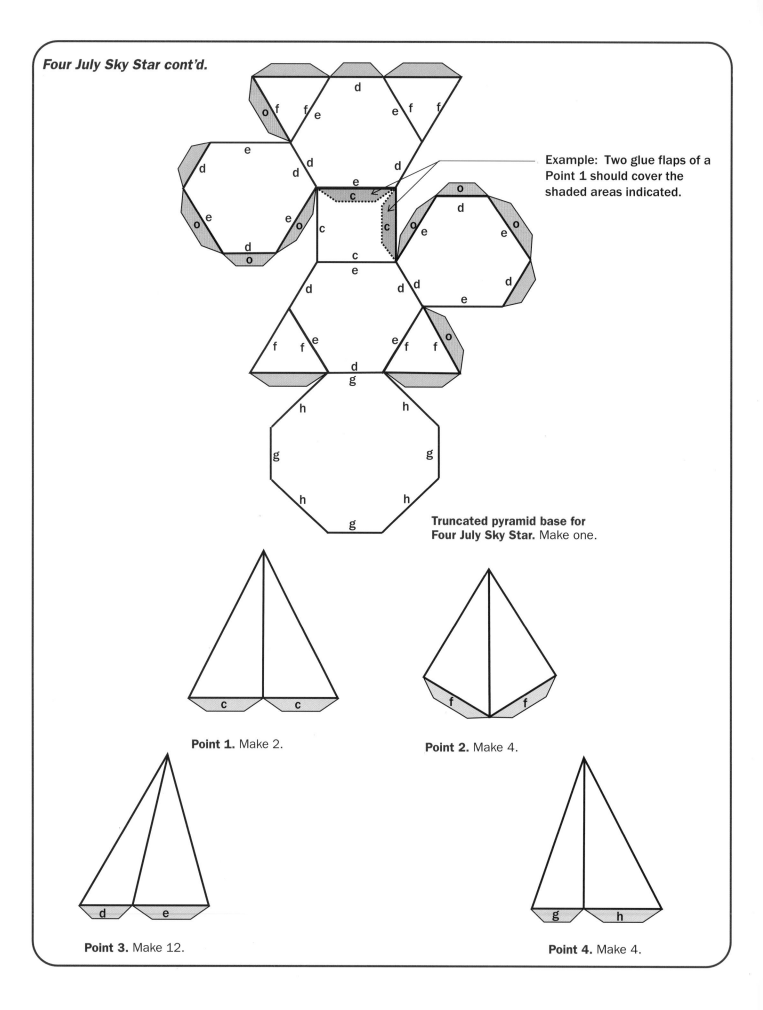

Four July Sky Star cont'd.

Example: Two glue flaps of a Point 1 should cover the shaded areas indicated.

Truncated pyramid base for Four July Sky Star. Make one.

Point 1. Make 2.

Point 2. Make 4.

Point 3. Make 12.

Point 4. Make 4.

Mira Ceti is a miraculous pulsating star that disappears and then reappears every 330 days.

1. Refer to the General Instructions section of the book for copying patterns. To make the icosahedron base, copy the base pattern to project paper and cut out the entire pattern, including the glue flaps. Fold on all black lines. Glue each unlabeled glue flap to its adjacent triangle. Complete and close the base by gluing the three c glue flaps to the three d edges. See the completed icosahedron base in Photo 1, left. You can keep the markings on the outside of the base as the points will entirely cover the base.

2. Make the 32 points: 2 regular pentagonal points, 10 trapezoidal points, 10 irregular pentagonal points, and 10 regular hexagonal points. After copying the point patterns to project paper, cut out each entire pattern, including the glue flaps. Fold on all lines. Complete each point by gluing flap a to its edge e.

3. Glue the 2 regular pentagonal points over two opposite corners of the base so that they cover the 2 purple areas. Attach the 10 irregular pentagonal points over the 10 white corners on the base, oriented so that the wider sides of the point (glue flaps w) are adjacent to the blue patches on the base. Attach the 10 trapezoidal points over the 10 blue trapezoids on the base. Orient so that the thin side of the point (with glue flap t) is adjacent to the pink patch on the base. Attach the 10 regular hexagonal points over the 10 pink hexagons on the base.

1. Icosahedron base and point.

2. The completed Mira Ceti.

3. Mira Ceti painted gold.

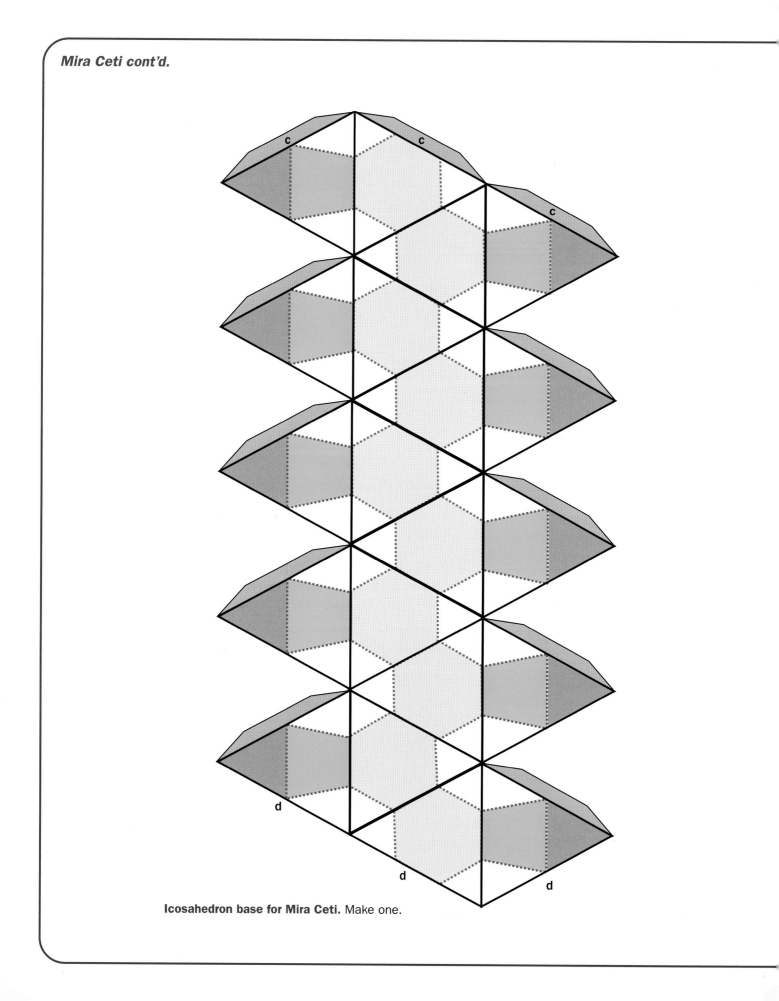

Icosahedron base for Mira Ceti. Make one.

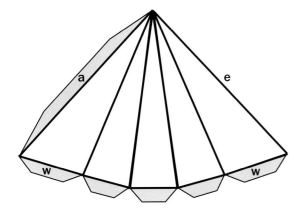

Irregular pentagonal point. Make 10.

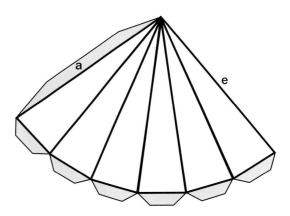

Regular hexagonal point. Make 10.

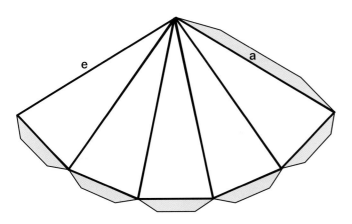

Regular pentagonal point. Make 2.

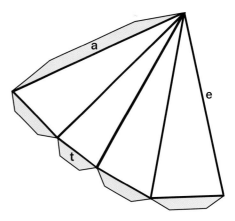

Trapezoidal point. Make 10.

Deimos is one of the moons of Mars, and this version definitely has lakes as well as mountains.

1. Icosidodecahedron base with one each of points 1, 2, 3, 4, and 5. Gray triangular areas in the base are openings.

1. Refer to the General Instructions section of the book for copying patterns. To make the base for Deimos, copy the base pattern to project paper and cut out the entire pattern, including the glue flaps. Fold on all lines. Attach each of the green glue flaps to its adjacent triangle. Attach each of the glue flaps labeled a, b, c, d, e, f, and g to the similarly labeled edge (flap a to edge a, etc.). When the base is finished, it will still have 8 triangular openings, as shown in Photo 1. This base is called an icosidodecahedron. It has 20 triangle faces and 12 pentagon faces.

2. Make the 28 points: 4 each of Point 1, 2, 3, and 4, and 12 of Point 5. For Points 1 and 2, put the colored side of the paper on the inside. For Points 3, 4, and 5, put it on the outside (see Photo 1). For each point, cut out the entire pattern, including the glue flaps. Fold on all lines. Complete each point by attaching glue flap a to the opposite edge e.

2. Base with Points 1 and 2 attached.

3. Attach the Point 1 and Point 2 points to the base. Each point is inserted into a triangular opening in the base, with the glue flaps attaching it on the outside of the base, as shown in Photo 2. These flaps will be covered up later. Point 1 points go into each of the triangular openings surrounded by blue lines on the base pattern, and Point 2 points go into each of the triangular openings surrounded by orange lines. These points form the lakes.

4. Glue the Point 3 points to the triangle faces labeled 3 on the base. Glue Point 4 points to the triangle faces labeled 4 on the base. Glue Point 5 points to the pentagon faces on the base. Note that 4 triangle faces of the base remain uncovered. These are the planes of Deimos.

3. The completed Deimos.

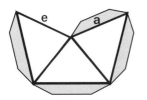

Point 1 and Point 3. Make 4 of each. Point 1 has the colored side of the paper on the inside. Point 3 has the colored side on the outside.

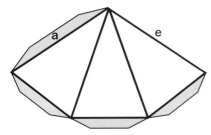

Point 2 and Point 4. Make 4 of each. Point 2 has colored side of paper on the inside. Point 4 has the colored side on the outside.

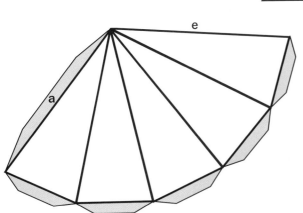

Point 5. Make 12.

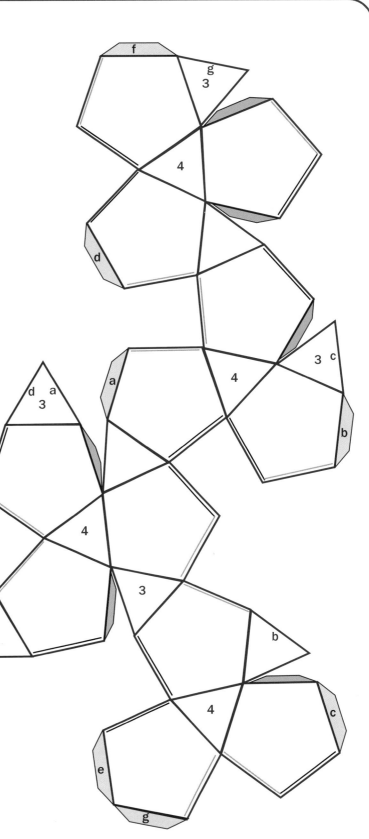

Icosidodecahedron base for Deimos. Make 1.

Emeralds have been sought for their beauty for thousands of years. Add this fanciful Emerald Star to your collection.

1. Refer to the General Instructions section of the book for copying patterns. To make the base, copy parts 1 and 2 of the base pattern to project paper, and cut out each entire pattern, including the glue flaps. Cut between the glue flaps and the adjacent shape where indicated by the red lines. Attach part 2 to part 1 by gluing flap m on part 1 to edge n on part 2. Fold the base on all lines. Attach each square to its adjacent heptagon (7-sided shape) using the gray glue flap. Next attach the hexagons to the adjacent shapes using all of the green g glue flaps. Now attach the 2 ends of the pattern together using the blue b glue flaps. Finally, close the figure by folding and gluing each of the 2 pentagons down onto the orange o glue flaps. See Photo 1 for the completed 32-sided base. This base is unique because it has 4-sided, 5-sided, 6-sided, and 7-sided faces.

2. To make the 32 points, copy the required number of each point pattern to project paper and cut out each entire pattern, including the glue flaps. Fold on all lines. Glue flap a to edge e on each point. Complete the tip of the point by using the glue flaps on the triangles to glue each triangle to the adjacent triangle.

3. Using the remaining glue flaps on each point, glue each square-edged (4-sided) point to a face on the base labeled 4. Glue each pentagonal (5-sided) point to a face labeled 5. Glue each hexagonal (6-sided) point to a face labeled 6, and each heptagonal (7-sided) point to a face labeled 7.

Try this project with red paper to make a ruby star.

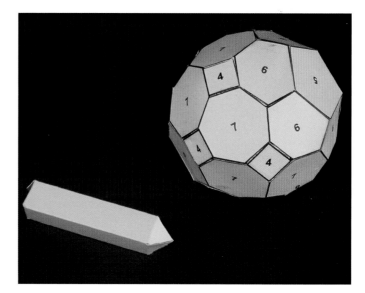

1. A square point and the 32-sided base.

2. The completed Emerald Star.

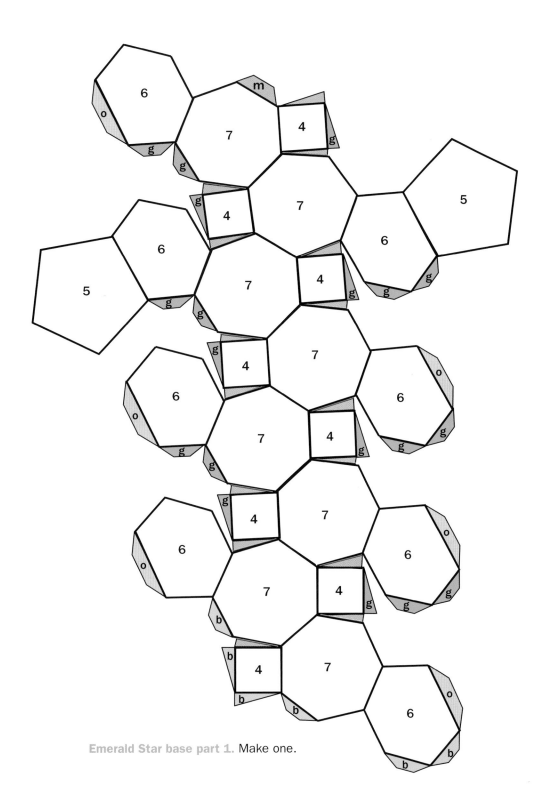

Emerald Star base part 1. Make one.

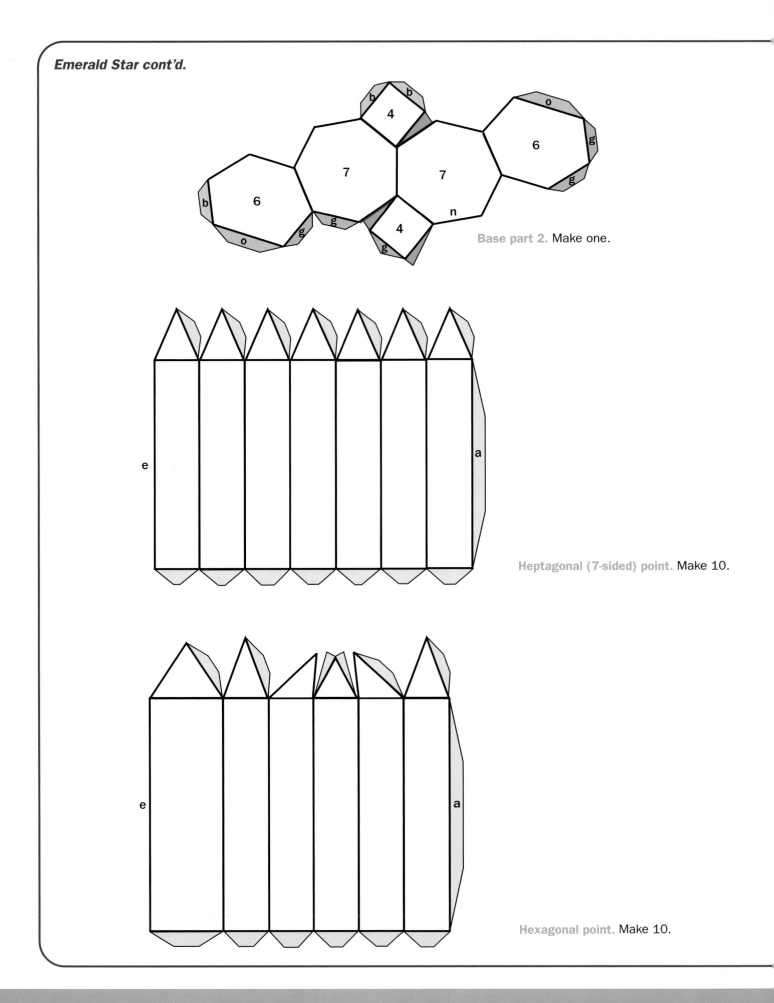

Base part 2. Make one.

Heptagonal (7-sided) point. Make 10.

Hexagonal point. Make 10.

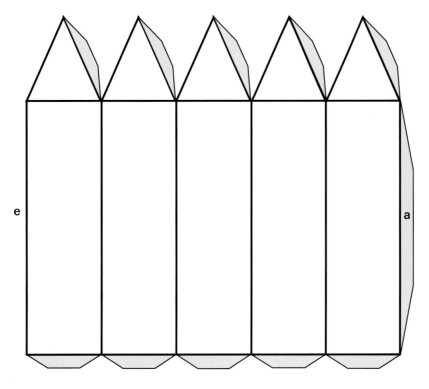

Pentagonal point. Make 2.

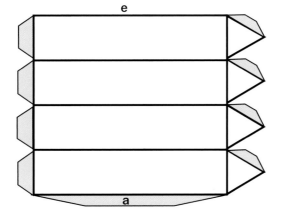

Square point. Make 10.

Are there parallel galaxies that overlap with our own galaxy? Make this project; then there will be at least one.

1. Refer to the General Instructions section of the book for copying patterns. Make the 3 oblique hexagonal prisms for the base: two of Prism 1 and one of Prism 2. After copying the patterns to project paper, cut out each entire pattern, including the glue flaps. Fold on all lines. Glue flap a to edge e. Next glue each triangle face to the adjacent parallelogram-shaped face using the blue b glue flaps. (A parallelogram is a 4-sided polygon whose opposite sides are parallel.) Complete and close each prism by gluing each of the rectangles down onto 3 yellow y glue flaps. Three completed oblique hexagonal prisms are shown in Photo 1.

2. To connect the 3 completed prisms to make the base, glue the pointy end of each of the Prism 1 prisms to the Prism 2 prism so that the pointy end touches at the red star on the Prism 2 prism pattern. Each Prism 1 prism should be glued to and cover a green-shaded area on the Prism 2 prism pattern. The 3 connected prisms should look as shown in Photo 2, right.

3. Make the 18 points: 9 of Point C and 9 of Point D. Copy each pattern to your project paper and cut out each entire pattern, including the glue flaps. Then cut on the red lines. Fold on all lines. Make the bend in the point by folding on the line between the 2 red-line cuts, sliding the upper side parts (above the red lines) under the lower side parts so that the z's of the upper parts end up on top of the x's. Glue the sides in this position. Color (with magic marker or paint) the back sides of the flaps on the points (the side that will show after gluing to the base) so that they are the same color as the base (seen in Photo 3). Each point now is bent like a bird's head and beak (see Photo 2).

4. Attach the points to the base: attach 3 of Point C and 3 of Point D to each prism of the base. For each point, glue the 3 point flaps (labeled f, g, and h or m, n, and o) along 3 edges of each parallelogram on the base, so that each flap is aligned along a similarly labeled line on the base (f covers f, etc.). Letters on base will not actually show, as they will be on the inside. See Photo 3 for reference.

1. Three completed oblique hexagonal prisms for the base.

2. Left to right: 2 points and the completed base.

3. The completed Parallel Universe.

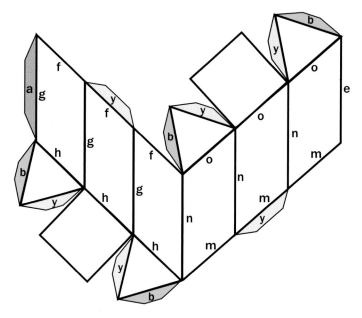

Oblique hexagonal prism 1 for the base of Parallel Universe. Make 2.

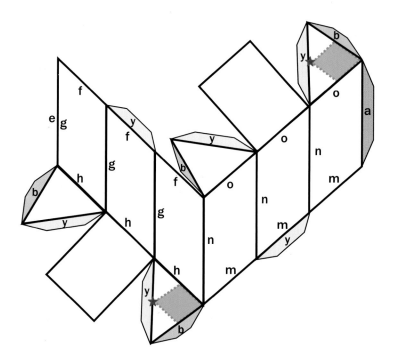

Oblique hexagonal prism 2 for the base. Make one.

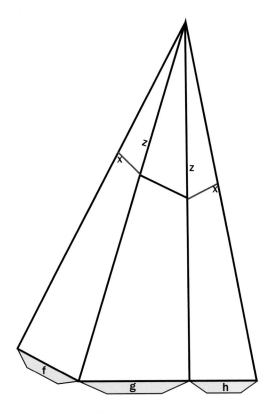

Point C. Make 9.

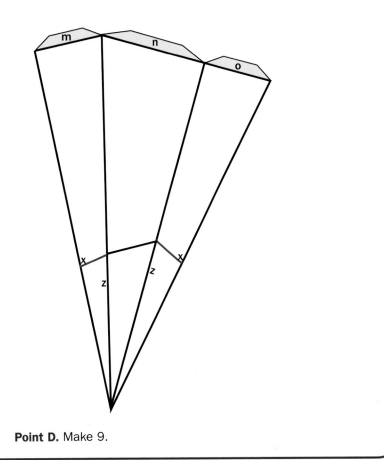

Point D. Make 9.

ANTI-GRAVITY SPACESHIP

The Anti-Gravity Spaceship is always ready for takeoff—always ready for you to take off writing with one of its pencils, that is, because it makes a neat pencil holder.

1. Refer to the General Instructions section of the book for copying patterns. A fairly stiff paper is the best choice for the base. This base is called an antiprism because it has identical top and bottom faces that are twisted with respect to each other and connected by alternating up-and-down triangles. First copy the patterns for base part 1 and base part 2 to your project paper, and cut out each entire pattern, including the glue flaps. Attach part 1 to part 2 by gluing flap m on part 2 to edge n on part 1. Use a small scissors to cut out the 5 small squares in the base top. Next fold the base on all lines. Partially assemble the base by gluing flap b to edge f and flap c to edge g.

2. Next add the inside pieces to the base. Cut the cardboard bottom pattern from thin cardboard and glue it to the bottom pentagon of the base (the pentagon without the cut-outs), as shown in Photo 1. The cardboard pentagon is slightly smaller than the base pentagon and should be centered on the base pentagon. Next copy to project paper and cut out 5 of the pencil tube pattern, including the flaps. Fold each into a tube, and then glue flap p to edge q. Use the remaining glue flaps on the pencil tube to attach each tube to the inner top of the base so the tube aligns under a small square cut-out. Glue the pencil tubes to the bottom of the base (to the cardboard) so that each tube is vertical (straight up and down).

3. To complete the antiprism base, close the base by gluing the remaining glue flaps on the triangle faces of the base to the top and bottom base pentagons, and glue flap w to edge x.

4. To make and attach the points, copy three of Point 1, two of Point 2, two of Point 3, two of Point 4, and one of Point 5 to project paper. Cut out the patterns, including the glue flaps. Fold on all lines. Complete each point by gluing its flap a to edge e. Use the remaining glue flaps on each point to attach the point to the base: glue each Point 1 to a triangle on the base labeled 1; glue each Point 2 to a triangle on the base labeled 2, etc.

1. Making the base. View of the cardboard bottom and pencil tubes.

2. The completed base.

3. The completed Anti-Gravity Spaceship.

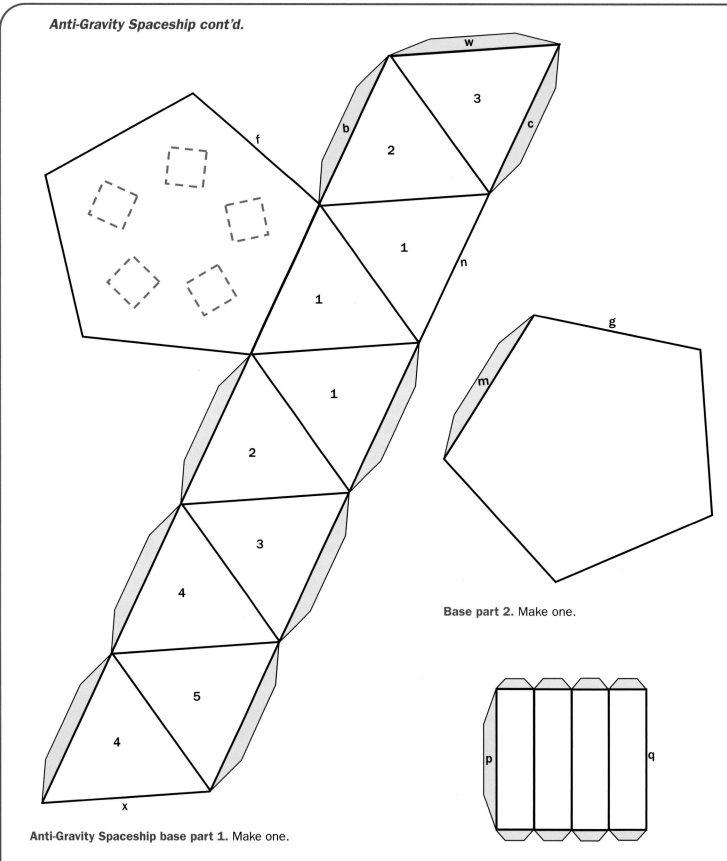

Anti-Gravity Spaceship base part 1. Make one.

Base part 2. Make one.

Pencil tube. Make 5.

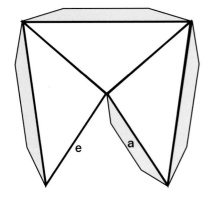

Point 1. Make 3.

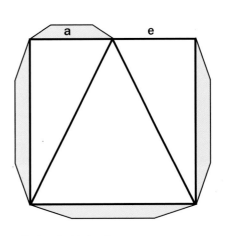

Point 2. Make 2.

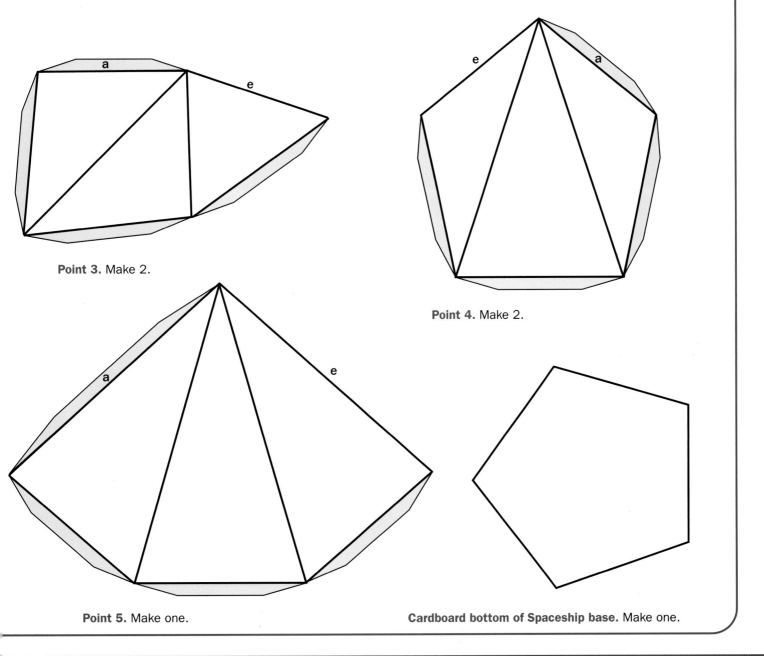

Point 3. Make 2.

Point 4. Make 2.

Point 5. Make one.

Cardboard bottom of Spaceship base. Make one.

The Celestial Intersection Star looks like 3 intersecting wedges.

1. Refer to the General Instructions section of the book for copying patterns. Try using a different color of paper for each of the 3 wedges. To make Wedge 1, copy the pattern to project paper and cut out the entire pattern, including the glue flaps. Cut between the yellow glue flaps and the main pattern on the red lines. Fold on all black lines. Connect each trapezoid to both of the adjacent trapezoids using the yellow glue flaps. Attach the glue flaps on the back side of the paper so they don't show. Then fold the wedge in half on the center line. With the remaining flaps folded to the inside of the wedge, glue flap a to flap b, glue flap c to flap d, and glue flap e to flap f. Photo 1 shows a complete Wedge 1 in the center.

2. Make two Wedge 2 halves and four Wedge 3 quarters. For each, copy the patterns to project paper and cut out the entire pattern, including the glue flaps. Cut between the yellow glue flaps and the main pattern on the red lines. Fold on all black lines. On each Wedge 2 half and Wedge 3 quarter, connect each trapezoid to the adjacent trapezoid using the yellow glue flaps. Fold the Wedge 2 half on the center line. Do the same for the Wedge 3 quarter. Glue flap a to flap b and (for Wedge 2 only) flap c to flap d so that the flaps end up on the inside of the wedge. Photo 1 shows a completed Wedge 2 half and Wedge 3 quarter.

3. Using the remaining glue flaps, glue on a Wedge 2 half so that it covers the blue area on the Wedge 1 pattern. You need to glue one Wedge 2 half on each side of Wedge 1. Trial-fit the pieces together before gluing, and make small adjustments to the location of the folds between the main pattern and the glue flaps if necessary to make a perfect fit. Photo 2 shows two Wedge 2 halves connected to Wedge 1.

4. To attach the four Wedge 3 quarters, use the remaining glue flaps to glue each Wedge 3 quarter so that it covers one of the 4 orange areas on Wedges 1 and 2. Trial-fit and adjust the folds between the glue flaps and the main pattern if needed to make a perfect fit.

1. Left to right: Wedge 2 half, Wedge, and Wedge 3 quarter.

2. Wedge 2 halves connected to Wedge 1.

3. The completed Celestial Intersection Star.

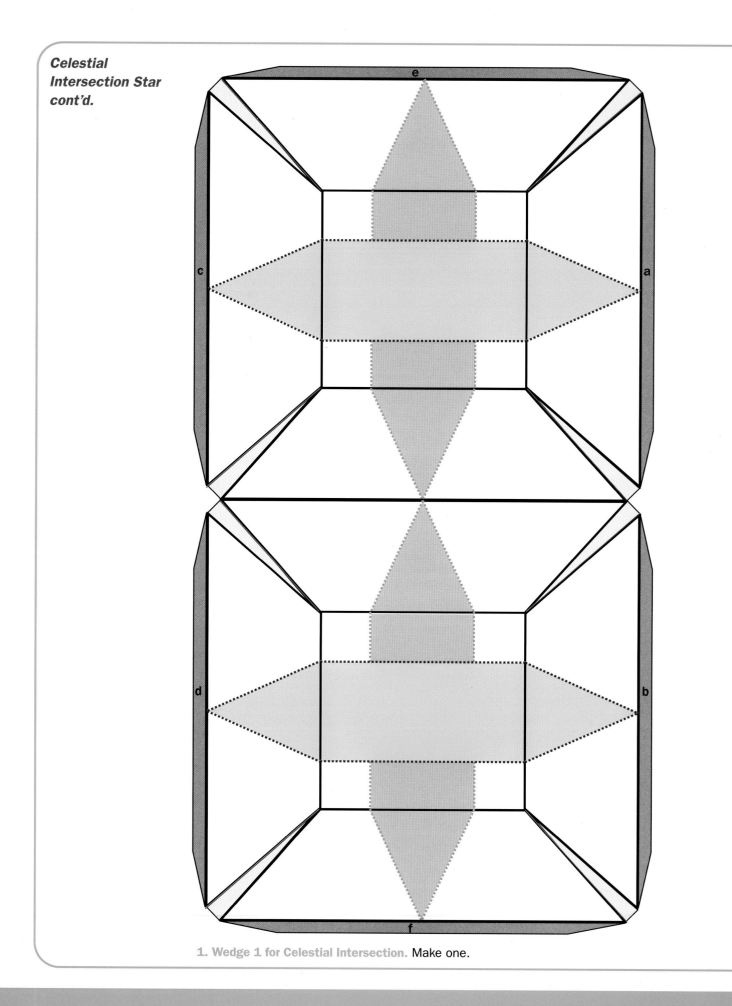

1. Wedge 1 for Celestial Intersection. Make one.

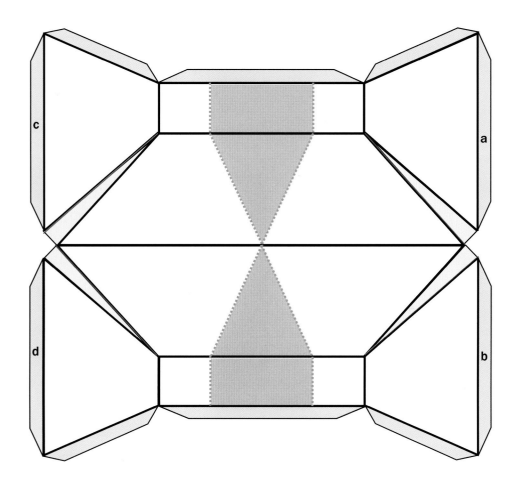

2. Wedge 2 half. Make 2.

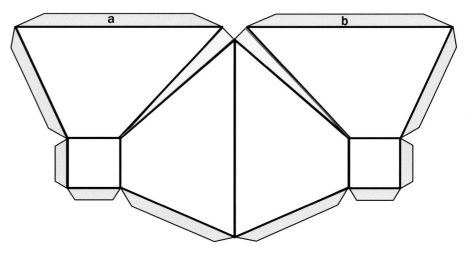

3. Wedge 3 quarter. Make 4.

If you could watch the entire world, you would see about 8 000 000 lightning flashes every day. Make it 8 000 001 with this Thunderbolt.

1. Refer to the General Instructions section of the book for copying patterns. To make the base, copy the pattern to project paper, and cut out the entire pattern, including the glue flaps. At the green glue flaps, cut between the glue flap and the hexagon or octagon, but leave the glue flap attached to the triangle. Fold on all lines. Use the green glue flaps to attach each triangle to the adjacent hexagon or octagon. Complete the base by attaching each remaining glue flap to the edge that has the same number or letter as the flap. This base is called a rhombitruncated cubeoctahedron. (Wow, what a name!) It is a polyhedron with 12 square faces, 8 hexagon faces, and 6 octagon faces. This one has slots on each of the square faces, as shown in Photo 1.

1. A completed point and base.

2. Make the 14 points: 8 hexagonal points and 6 octagonal points. Copy the patterns to project paper and cut out each entire pattern, including the glue flaps. Fold on all black lines. Unfold. Cut away the cut-outs on each point (3 on the hexagonal point and 4 on the octagonal point) by cutting on the green dashed lines. Refold and attach glue flap a to edge e on each point.

3. To attach the points to the base, glue each hexagonal point to a hexagonal face and each octagonal point to an octagonal face. Attaching points is easier if you glue 2 adjacent glue flaps to the base and let them dry. Then glue the remaining glue flaps.

2. The completed Thunderbolt.

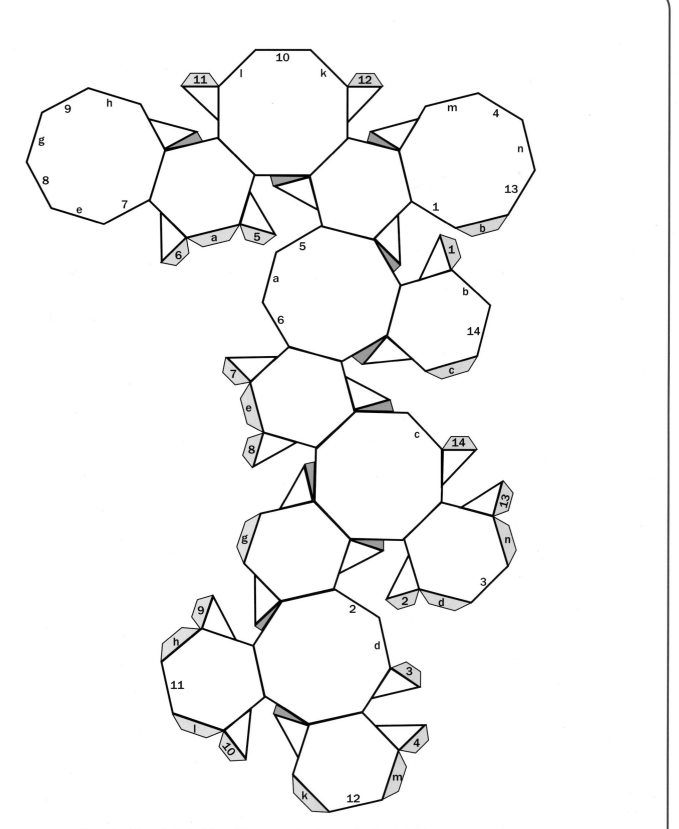

Base for Thunderbolt (rhombitruncated cubeoctahedron). Make one.

3. A lighted Thunderbolt.

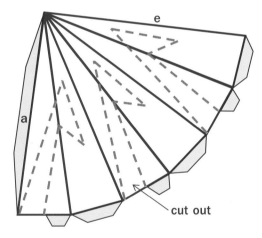

Hexagonal point. Make 8.

cut out

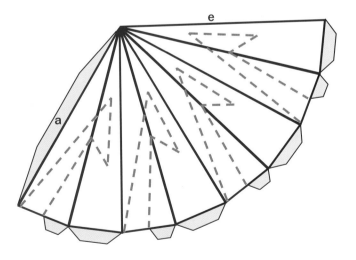

Octagonal point. Make 6.

Radiation from the Trapezium quadruple star causes the Orion Nebula to glow. Create your own glow with this Trapezium project.

1. Refer to the General Instructions section of the book for copying patterns. To make the octahedron base, start by making 8 of the base part: 4 of one color and 4 of another. Copy the pattern to project paper and cut out each entire pattern, including the glue flaps. Fold on all solid lines (not on the dotted lines). Glue the base parts together flap to flap, with 4 triangles coming together at each point. The two colors can be arranged so that each triangle is attached to a triangle of the other color at each of its 3 edges. The finished base octahedron should look as shown in Photo 1 (like 2 square-based pyramids attached at the base).

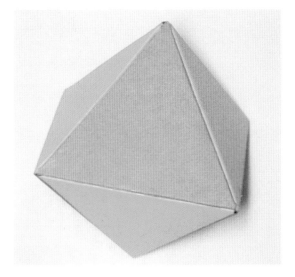

1. The octahedron base.

2. Make the 24 points, 12 from each of the 2 paper colors used for the base. Copy the pattern to project paper and cut out each entire pattern, including the glue flaps. Fold on all lines. For each point, glue flap a to edge e to complete the point. Points should look as shown in Photo 2.

3. Attach 3 points to each face of the base, using the remaining point glue flaps. Place each point within the triangular area outlined with dotted lines on the base part pattern. The base will still be visible through the points, so attach each point to a base face of the same color as the point. The corner of each point with the 2 small blue circles should be at the center of the base face, at the location marked with a blue circle on the base.

2. Points.

3. The completed Trapezium.

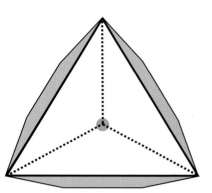

Base part of Trapezium. Make 8.

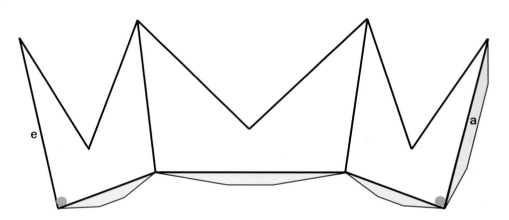

Point. Make 24.

4. Another view of the Trapezium.

WORMHOLE

Take a shortcut through space and time.
Enter the Wormhole if you dare.

1. Refer to the General Instructions section of the book for copying patterns. Both sides of the paper will be visible, so keep this in mind when choosing paper. You will need to make 12 tunnels: 6 of Tunnel 1 and 6 of Tunnel 2. Copy the patterns to project paper and cut out each entire pattern, including the glue flap. Fold on all black lines. Complete each tunnel by gluing flap a to edge e.

2. The tunnels are connected end to end like a train, by gluing the small end of one tunnel into the large end of the previous tunnel (see photos). Tunnel types are alternated: Tunnel 1, Tunnel 2, Tunnel 1, Tunnel 2, etc. Glue each tunnel so that its blue pattern area covers the green-shaded area on the previous tunnel. Continue until all 12 tunnels are connected to form the spiraled Wormhole.

1. One tunnel and two connected tunnels.

2. The completed Wormhole.

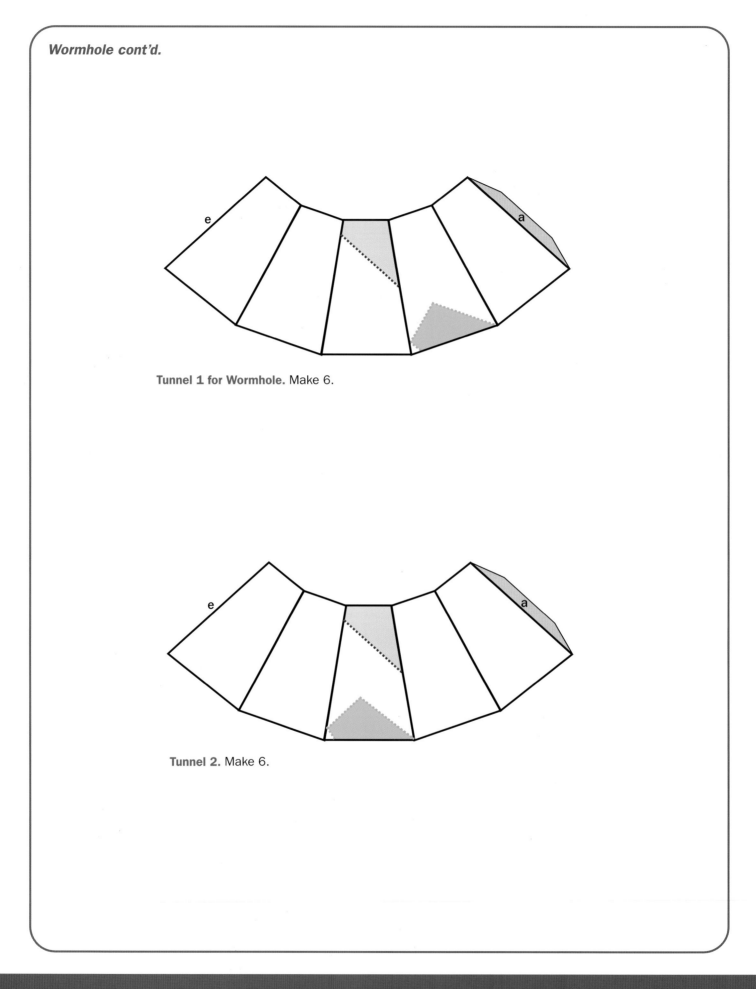

Tunnel 1 for Wormhole. Make 6.

Tunnel 2. Make 6.

SQUASHED CUBES

Four cubes squashed together? Looks like that's how it was made, but this pattern will show you an easier way.

1 to 3. Steps 1 to 3 are the same as those for the Tetra-Twelve project. Use the Tetra-Twelve base (page 14) and intermediate tetrahedron patterns and follow Steps 1, 2, and 3 of the Tetra-Twelve project to make the base tetrahedron and attach the 4 intermediate tetrahedrons.

4. Make 12 points using the new pattern given here. Copy and cut out the entire point, and fold on all lines. Complete each point by gluing flap a to the opposite triangle at edge e. Each point will make a corner of one of the cubes.

5. Attach a point to each face of the intermediate tetrahedrons, using the remaining glue flaps on each point.

You can mix colors on each cube, as shown in Photo 1, or each cube can be made in one color by making all three points on each intermediate tetrahedron the same color as their intermediate tetrahedron, as shown in Photo 2.

2. The completed Squashed Cubes with one red cube, one blue cube, one silver cube, and one gold cube.

1. The completed Squashed Cubes with white, gray-patterned, and silver paper.

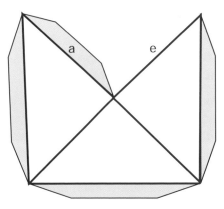

Point. Make 12 for Squashed Cube.

Looks like chaos, but look again; it has a perfectly organized pattern and geometry.

1. Refer to the General Instructions section of the book for copying patterns. A fairly stiff paper, like card stock, works well for this project. Both sides of the paper will show. To make the 18 petals, copy the pattern to project paper and cut out each entire pattern, including the glue flap. Fold on the lines between the house-shaped faces (pentagons) on the pattern; fold so that the lines are on the outside. For each petal, glue flap a to edge e. Fold each of the small thin triangles on the petals to the outside. A completed petal should look as shown in Photo 1, right.

2. Connect 8 of the petals in a ring. Glue a house-shaped face on one petal to a house-shaped face on the next petal, until the ring is completed as shown Photo 1, left.

3. With the ring of petals laid horizontally as shown in Photo 1, make another ring of petals that is a vertical ring. This ring will include the two petals marked with an x on Photo 1. To do this, connect three new petals (house-to-house) in a row and then attach this assembly to the upper side of the two petals marked with an x to make the upper half of the ring (see Photo 2; the three new petals are labeled 3). Connect three more new petals in a row and attach this assembly to the lower side of the two petals marked x to form the lower half of the ring.

4. Add another vertical ring of petals. This ring will include the two petals marked with an o in Photo 1 and Photo 2. This ring will also include the upper and lower petals on the first vertical ring. It is built by attaching one petal above and below each horizontal petal labeled o in Photo 1 and also attaching these four new petals to the upper and lower petals on the first vertical ring.

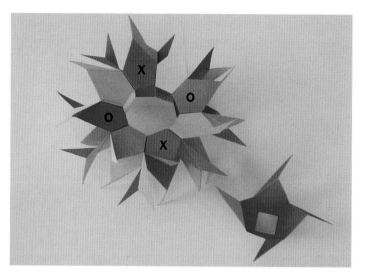

1. A completed petal (lower right) and eight petals in a ring.

2. With upper half of the first vertical ring added.

In the end, the petals are arranged the same as the square faces on a rhombicubeoctahedron (see Cimmerian Night project).

3. The completed Galactic Chaos, with 6 pink petals and 12 orange petals.

4. Another view of the completed Galactic Chaos.

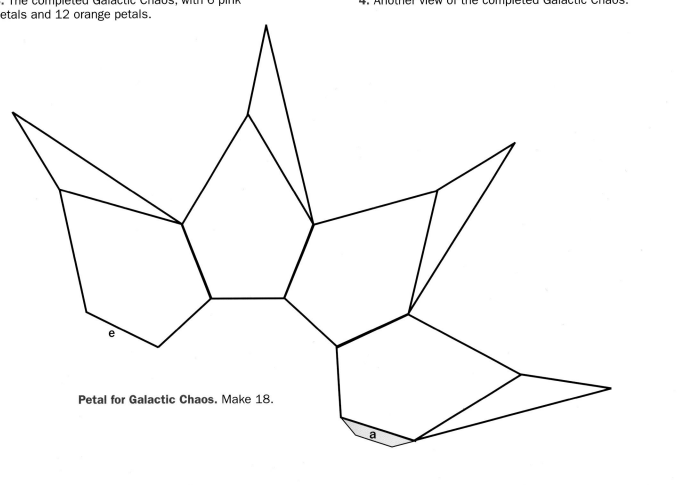

Petal for Galactic Chaos. Make 18.

Thinking of visiting a friend in the next galaxy? Better buy a ticket for the Interstellar Cruise Ship.

1. Refer to the General Instructions section of the book for copying patterns. To make the ship sides, copy 4 of the ship side pattern to project paper and cut out the entire patterns, including the glue flaps. Glue c flaps on the first side piece to edge d on the second side piece. Glue c flaps on the second side piece to edge d on the third side piece. Glue c flaps on the third side piece to edge d on the fourth side piece. Fold on all lines. The long lines between the trapezoids should be folded in valley and mountain folds (see page 48 for diagram of those folds) so that the sides will fit onto the front and back; see Photo 1. Then glue c flaps on the fourth side piece to edge d on the first side piece.

2. Make one of the ship front; copy to the same project paper as used for the sides, and cut out pattern. Attach ship front to the ship sides by gluing it to the f flaps on the sides. Glue three f flaps at a time, and hold them in place until the glue dries. Then do the next three f glue flaps, etc., until the front is completely connected.

3. Make one of the ship back; copy it to the same project paper as used for the sides, and cut out pattern. Attach the ship back to the ship sides by gluing it to the b flaps on the sides. Glue three b flaps at a time and hold until glue dries; then do the next three b glue flaps, etc., until the back is completely connected.

4. Make 3 nose cones. For each, copy the nose cone pattern to the same project paper as used for the sides and cut out the entire pattern, including the glue flaps. Fold on all lines. Glue flap o to edge n. Attach the nose cones to the ship by using the remaining nose cone glue flaps to attach a nose cone to each of the octagons on the ship front.

5. Make 4 flames. For each, copy the flame pattern to project paper (try orange or blue paper) and cut out the entire pattern, including the glue flaps. Fold on all lines. Glue flap a to edge e. Attach to ship by using the remaining flame glue flaps to attach a flame to each of the squares on the ship back.

6. Decorate by adding windows, hatches, lights, or whatever you like.

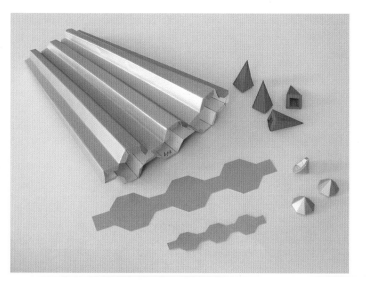

1. Upper left: Sides connected and folded. Front row: Ship's front and back. At right: 4 flames and 3 nose cones.

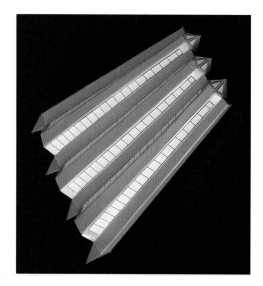

2. The completed Interstellar Cruise Ship.

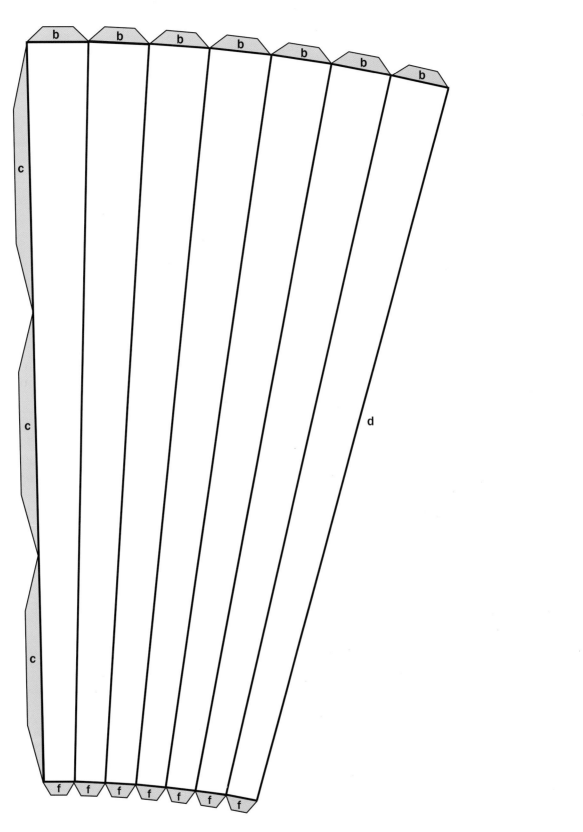

Ship side piece for Interstellar Cruise Ship. Make 4.

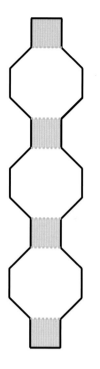

Ship front. Make 1.

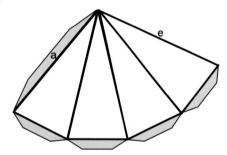

Flame. Make 4.

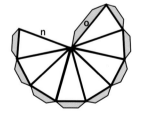

Nose cone. Make 3.

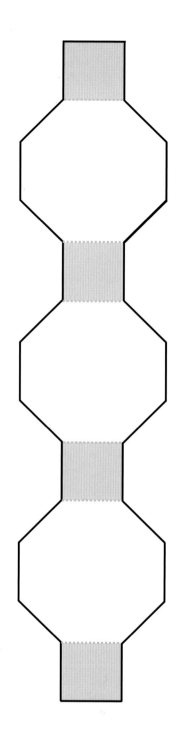

Ship back. Make 1

ASTEROID

There are more than 7000 asteroids orbiting the Sun in a giant asteroid belt between Mars and Jupiter. Some are as small as boulders; the largest is more than 500 miles across. Add another small one with this Asteroid project.

1. Refer to the General Instructions section of the book for copying patterns. This asteroid is a cubeoctahedron. Copy the pattern to project paper and cut out the entire pattern, including the glue flaps. Fold on all lines. Unfold and lay flat. Cut small, randomly spaced holes in each face using a scissor or by punching with a hand-held hole punch (the type used to punch holes for putting paper into a 3-ring binder). Photo 1 shows how the asteroid will look after this step.

2. Refold on lines. Glue the 5 green g glue flaps to the adjacent triangles.

3. Wad a piece of paper into a ball of a size that will just fit inside of the partly constructed asteroid in Step 2. The outside of this wadded-up ball will show through the holes on the outside of your asteroid.

4. Complete and close the asteroid by gluing the remaining 6 glue flaps to the adjacent triangles.

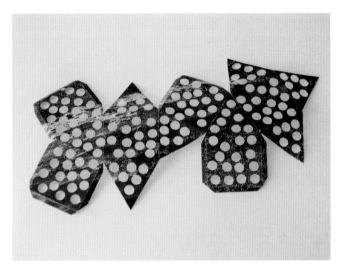

1. Asteroid after cutting or punching small holes in each face of the cubeoctahedron.

2. The completed Asteroid.

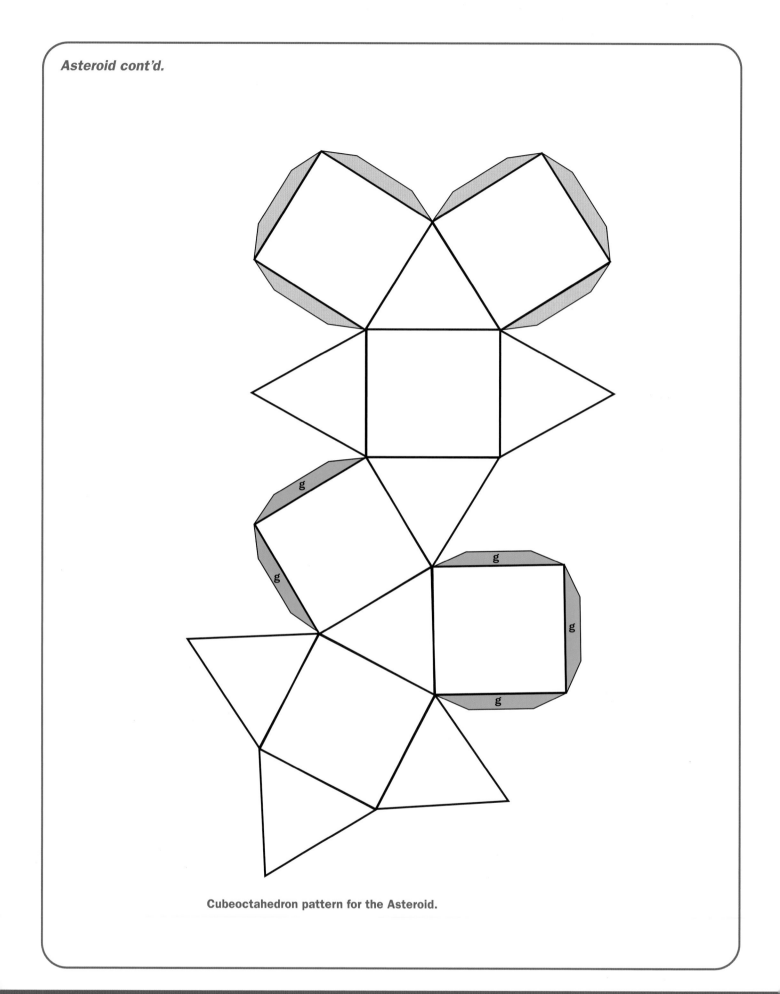

Cubeoctahedron pattern for the Asteroid.

Base Geometry Summary

The projects in the book are built using many different geometric shapes. A list and description of the base shapes is provided below. All are polyhedrons except the last one on the list (14-circle).

The first 5 bases are also known as the 5 Platonic solids. On a Platonic solid, all faces are identical regular polygons, and the same number of faces meet at each vertex. A regular polygon is a shape with straight sides, all of which are of equal length; all the angles in a regular polygon are equal to each other.

The next 6 bases listed are 6 of the 13 Archimedean solids. On an Archimedean solid, all faces are regular polygons (but they are not all identical polygons), and the same number of each type of face meet at each vertex.

Base Types and Their Characteristics

Tetrahedron: 4 triangle faces, 6 edges, 4 vertices

Cube (hexahedron): 6 tetragon faces; 12 edges, 8 vertices

Octahedron: 8 triangle faces; 12 edges, 6 vertices

Dodecahedron: 12 pentagon faces, 30 edges, 20 vertices

Icosahedron: 20 triangle faces, 30 edges, 12 vertices

Cubeoctahedron: 8 triangle faces, 6 tetragon faces, 24 edges, 12 vertices

Rhombicube-octahedron: 8 triangle faces, 18 tetragon faces, 48 edges, 24 vertices

Rhombitruncated cubeoctahedron: 12 tetragon faces, 8 hexagon faces, 6 octagon faces, 72 edges, 48 vertices

Truncated icosahedron: 12 pentagon faces, 20 hexagon faces, 90 edges, 60 vertices

Truncated octahedron: 6 tetragon faces, 8 hexagon faces, 36 edges, 24 vertices

Icosidodecahedron: 20 triangle faces, 12 pentagon faces, 60 edges, 30 vertices

Hexagonal pyramid: 6 triangle faces, 1 hexagon face, 12 edges, 7 vertices

Truncated square pyramid: 4 triangle faces, 1 tetragon face, 4 hexagon faces, 1 octagon face, 24 edges, 16 vertices

Pentagonal prism: 5 tetragon faces, 2 pentagon faces, 15 edges, 10 vertices

Hexagonal prism: 6 tetragon faces, 2 hexagon faces, 18 edges, 12 vertices

Oblique hexagonal prism: 4 triangle faces, 8 tetragon faces, 22 edges, 12 vertices

Truncated octagonal prism: 14 tetragon faces, 28 edges, 16 vertices

Pentagonal anti-prism: 10 triangle faces, 2 pentagon faces, 20 edges, 10 vertices

Double tetrahedron: 6 triangle faces, 9 edges, 5 vertices

Square wedge: 10 tetragon faces, 20 edges, 12 vertices

24-triangle: also called 24-sided base; 24 triangle faces, 36 edges, 14 vertices

4-5-6-7 solid: also called 32-sided base; 10 tetragon faces, 2 pentagon faces, 10 hexagon faces, 10 heptagon faces, 90 edges, 60 vertices

Pentagon-hexagonal toroid: 30 tetragon faces, 60 edges, 30 vertices

14-circle: 14 circle faces

Index